IN GOD'S COMMUNITY

Essays on the Church and Its Ministry

Edited by David J. Ellis
and W. Ward Gasque

Harold Shaw Publishers
Wheaton, Illinois

IN GOD'S COMMUNITY
The Church and Its Ministry
© 1978 by Pickering & Inglis Ltd.
ISBN 0 7208 041 16

Published in the United States of America as
IN GOD'S COMMUNITY: Essays on the
Church and Its Ministry
by special arrangement with Pickering & Inglis, Ltd.,
Glasgow

First Printing, 1979

Library of Congress Cataloging in Publication Data
Main entry under title:

In God's community.

  Bibliography: p.
  Includes indexes.
  1. Church–Addresses, essays, lectures.   2. Clergy
–Office–Addresses, essays, lectures.   3. Mission of
the Church–Addresses, essays, lectures.   I. Ellis,
David J.   II. Gasque, W. Ward.
BV600.2.I5   260   79-12847
ISBN 0-87788-392-0

Printed in the United States of America

To
GEORGE CECIL DOUGLAS HOWLEY

*With appreciation
and deep affection
in the Lord*

Contents

Preface

Each generation of Christians has the obligation to think through the teaching of Scripture for itself. It must not be content with simply repeating the words of previous generations; rather, it must seek to freshly appropriate God's Word and to translate it into terms meaningful to the age in which it lives. If it does end up eventually making use of similar words to those used by previous generations, it must be because it has found this way of expressing the truth of God to be faithful to Scripture rather than simply familiar-sounding and therefore comfortable, for it is Scripture that is the ultimate authority—not tradition (whether ancient or modern).

The following collection of essays represents an attempt to take a fresh look at Scripture and to see what it has to teach concerning the doctrine of the church and what lessons might be drawn for the life of the church today. The present volume bears comparison to an earlier work, *The Church: A Symposium* (Pickering & Inglis, 1949), edited by J. B. Watson. That volume attempted to do exactly what we have tried to do in this one; and like the sixteen authors of the earlier work, the present authors are all associated with assemblies of Christian Brethren. We write, therefore, from within the context of a particular fellowship of God's people, though it is to be hoped that we do not reflect a sectarian point of view and that what we have written will be of interest and perhaps even also of some help to Christians of other fellowships.

It is customary for professional academics who have made significant contributions to scholarship and also some impression on a new generation of scholars to receive a *Festschrift*, a volume of essays written in their honour by a group of former students and colleagues. But it is much rarer for one who has been primarily a churchman to be thus honoured, even when he has made an equal or even greater impact upon the life of the church and its leadership. When the two editors conceived of the idea of gathering a contemporary collection of essays on the subject of the church and its ministry, it immediately seemed appropriate to think of dedicating it to our esteemed friend and Editor of *The Witness*, G. C. D. Howley. Not only has he been of great help and encouragement to both of us, but he has also been used of God to the benefit of many younger men and women who have sought to serve the Lord in various parts of the world. There has been no one, we believe, in the Brethren movement who has given more encouragement to our generation, and there have been few in any church fellowship who have made such a widespread impression for good on so many. It therefore gives us a great deal of pleasure to be able to so dedicate this symposium.

The doctrine of the church is an area where many real and deep cleavages continue to exist among Christians, in spite of all the talk concerning church unity that has marked our day. Christian opinion is often shaped more by tradition than by the Bible, whether these traditions be centuries old or merely a few decades. We recognize that some of what has been written in the pages which follow will tend to challenge some of these traditions. However, with the editor of *The Church: A Symposium*, 'We would only venture to ask that the chapters be read with Holy Writ as their testing standard and that a spirit of patience may prevail in regard to any criticism or in respect to points of difference.'

D.J.E.
W.W.G.

George Cecil Douglas Howley:

An Appreciation

F. F. BRUCE

To write about a personal friend is a much more difficult task than to write about some figure in history or some contemporary theologian whom one knows from his published works rather than as a man. Yet the task must be assayed, and while I am fully conscious of its difficulty I am conscious also of a sense of gratitude that I should be the one invited to undertake it.

My acquaintance with Cecil Howley goes back forty-five years, to a time when we were youngsters in our twenties. Since this is a personal appreciation and not a biography I need say nothing of his life and development before I knew him; it is a subject into which I have conducted no research, although I gather that his early environment was quite different from mine. When I first met him, he had already begun to cultivate a remarkable gift for the oral exposition of Scripture. From time to time he was a visiting speaker at Panton Hall, Cambridge, where I worshipped during my student years in that city, and I quickly recognized in him a man whose principles of biblical interpretation were closely similar to mine. He was concerned to bring out the plain meaning of the words in their literary and historical context, leaving typology and allegorization to others (and we had more of those 'others' then than we have now).

After I left Cambridge we did not meet for several years. When we did meet again, I was living in Leeds, and had opportunities of seeing and hearing him when he visited Yorkshire. By then he was giving his whole time to the ministry and also (and more importantly) he had married a wife—about whom more anon. He stayed with us several times both in Leeds and in Sheffield, after we moved there, and was always a welcome guest because he fitted in to our domestic set-up and made himself at home. He showed a lively and unaffected interest in our two children, as I am assured he has done in the children of other homes where he has stayed. There used to be (it is said) two awkward categories of visiting preachers: those who ignored the presence of children altogether and (even worse) those who pestered them with embarrassingly personal questions. Our guest fitted into neither of these categories; all of us felt when he left that it would be pleasant to have him back again.

It was a tremendous occasion for him when, early in 1949, he acquired a son of his own. Later that year J. B. Watson added a postscript to a letter which he sent to me on some matter connected with *The Witness*: 'Have you observed the new note of authority that has crept into our friend Cecil's voice of late?' Peter indeed provided great joy to both his parents, and their joy was doubled a few years later when Robert came to join him.

In those years Cecil's ministry was becoming ever more widely appreciated—not only throughout Great Britain and Ireland but overseas too. Australia and New Zealand, Canada and the United States were among the countries where he became personally known. In my own travels abroad I meet people in one city after another who speak in the warmest terms of Cecil Howley and beg me to give him their love on my return home. Perhaps his travels abroad taught him one lesson even more effectively than his ministry in the British Isles had done: that it is impossible to please everybody. The Bible is full of controversial material, and its interpretation is an exercise further beset by controversy. There is one type of Bible reader who feels uneasy or affronted when he finds that others take a different view of its meaning from his own, and cannot rest until he persuades them to agree with him. Cecil Howley, being an independent thinker, frequently holds and expounds views which are not at all in line with the traditions to which his hearers have been accustomed; and sometimes his hearers, instead of imitating the men of Beroea and searching the Scriptures to see if these things are so, object to being confronted with views different from what they have always been taught. His own reaction is to spell out his arguments and demonstrate his conclusions with added clarity, so that no one can be mistaken about what he believes or why he believes it.

In 1955 he entered on a new phase of biblical ministry. For some time, during J. B. Watson's last illness, he had given him help with the editing of *The Witness*; and with his death in that year Cecil Howley was the obvious man to succeed him in the editorial chair. A week or two after the announcement of the new appointment our friend Howard Mudditt remarked to me: 'So Cecil is editor of *The Witness*. Plymouth Brother Number One!' I don't suppose that any editor of *The Witness* ever envisaged himself in that last role, but while the words were spoken in jest they reflect the influence and prestige which the editorship has carried with it since the journal was founded in 1871. However, the words might also convey an impression of sectarianism quite out of keeping with Cecil's character. His ecumenical interests and activities are in the best tradition of the pioneers of the Brethren movement; one has only to think in this connexion of his active participation in the work of the Evangelical Alliance. His editorship lasted until the end of 1977, and even since then 'Touchstone' essays from his pen have continued to appear in *The Witness*.

Over these years he gave *The Witness* a new look and kept its pages abreast of matters of current interest. On issues where there was diversity of opinion within the constituency of the journal he was ever careful not to promote one particular line, not even that which he himself favoured. Certainly under his editorship greater variety of viewpoint found expression in *The Witness* than in earlier days. Another feature of *The Witness* is closely related to one of Cecil Howley's greatest virtues. He has been over the years a great encourager of young men and women, and quite a number of younger writers have appeared for the first time in print in *The Witness*. The same feature is evident in another of his editorial enterprises, *A New Testament Commentary*. One reviewer of this work wondered aloud who chose the contributors—a pointless question for someone who knows what an editor's function is—but the fact was that some of them were younger men whose names were relatively unknown until this *Commentary* brought them before the public eye. But Cecil Howley had discerned their qualities and decided that participation in this work was what was necessary to bring those qualities to greater maturity.

As an editor he was meticulously conscientious. Not a word escaped his scrutiny; everything was carefully weighed before it was passed for publication. This does not mean that everything had to command the editor's agreement: he knew an editor's business better than that! Shortly after J. B. Watson succeeded to the editorship of *The Witness* in 1941 he said, 'The surest way to make enemies is to become an editor'—either by not publishing what readers would like him to publish (especially their own offerings) or by publishing what readers would prefer to be left unpublished. If Mr Watson felt like that, so did his successor. Cecil Howley has many excellent qualifications for editorship; he has only one disqualification—the lack of an extra-thick skin. He is particularly sensitive to criticism, not to reasonable criticism but to the offensive kind which some people confuse with faithfulness to the truth, and he is treated to more than his fair share of the latter kind. Yet the appreciation of an increasing number of readers outweighs the depreciation expressed by the few.

The *New Testament Commentary* was an immense undertaking; it occupied nine years from its first beginnings to its publication in 1969. As one of the consulting editors I am in a better position than most to know something of the care and toil which, during that time, the editor-in-chief devoted to each one of its 666 pages. The widespread commendation with which it was greeted when it appeared was compensation for the time and labour which he bestowed on it. He is now engaged in the final stages of editing a companion work covering the Old Testament.

No tribute to Cecil Howley would be complete if a generous place were not given to his magnificent wife for her substantial contribution to the man he is and the work he has accomplished. Robina might not agree entirely with the sentiment once expressed to my wife by the late Mrs Rendle Short: 'My dear, we *are* our husbands'—but Cecil would readily acknowledge that where Robina is concerned there is much truth in it. Throughout their years together she has given him all the encouragement and support that he has needed, and outstandingly so in these most recent years, when he had to suffer an amputation which might have been as psychologically crippling as it was physically crippling. The spirit with which he has set himself to triumph over this disability has won the admiration of his friends; they see in it a token of his personal faith and resolution, but they also see in it evidence of Robina's love and care in very trying circumstances. Instead of giving way to the depression which many a wife might naturally have felt in such a situation, she has manifested a serenity and cheerfulness which must have been an incalculable help to him. To say more would embarrass them both, but what has been said is well recognized by all their friends to be the plain truth.

The pattern of his life has had to be modified, but he shows no abatement of activity, although more of it is carried on at his desk and in Montpelier Church, Purley, than was formerly so. In their happy home books, music and love abound. With all that, and the presence of God to crown it, what more could one desire? Cecil and Robina, this book bespeaks our grateful affection for you both. All the contributors, and very many others right round the world, rejoice that our lives have been enriched by your friendship. Grace and peace be with you!

1

The Church in the New Testament

W. WARD GASQUE

Meaning of Ekklēsia

The English word 'church' comes into our language via the German and Latin from the Greek *kyriakon*, meaning 'that which belongs to the Lord'. Originally, it was an adjective motifying *dōma* or *oikia*, signifying 'the Lord's house' or a place of Christian worship, hence our use of church for a building in which Christians gather to worship their Lord. Thus our word 'church' derives from a post-biblical usage. The word *ekklēsia* in the New Testament, normally translated by 'church', is never used to indicate a building; rather, it always refers to people.

To the ordinary reader of the English Bible, 'church' is exclusively a New Testament word. To the early Christians, who read both the Old and New Testaments in Greek, this was not so. In fact, *ekklēsia* occurs nearly a hundred times in the Septuagint—just a few times less than in the New Testament. It is the translation of the Hebrew word *qāhāl*, a term used most often in the Old Testament to signify the people of God gathered together in assembly before the LORD (Deut. 4:10; 9:10; 18:16; Ps. 22:22 [quoted in Heb. 2:12]; II Chr. 30:13; cf. Acts 7:38). Thus it seems unlikely that an early Christian would consider the church as a totally New Testament phenomenon, though he would recognize that a new and fuller meaning was poured into the term by the coming of the Lord Jesus Christ and the subsequent gift of the Holy Spirit. Rather, he would see in the use of the term *ekklēsia* one of many links between the Old Testament and

1

the New indicating an essential continuity between the old Israel and the new.

In secular Greek of New Testament times the word *ekklēsia* meant simply a gathering or meeting of any kind. It could refer to a regularly constituted political assembly (as it does in Acts 19:39) or to an ordinary meeting (as in the case of the mob who surged into the theatre in Ephesus, Acts 19:32,40). In view of the root meaning of the term (from a verb meaning 'to call out') it has been often suggested that the basic meaning in the New Testament of *ekklēsia* is to signify 'a called out people' with a strong emphasis upon separation from the surrounding world. There is however no evidence to show that the term as used by the New Testament writers has strong connotations of its original etymological meaning; rather, it seems to carry with it the connotation of its Old Testament association with *qāhāl*, God's people assembled to worship and serve Him. If there is a special emphasis in the New Testament use of *ekklēsia* beyond this, it is upon *a gathering to* (the Lord) rather than upon a calling out. The church in the New Testament is the assembly of believers who have been drawn together through Jesus Christ for the purpose of worshipping, serving and obeying God in the world in the power of the Holy Spirit. The mission of the church is not that of withdrawing from the world but of witness to the world, not of separation but of proclamation.

The Church In the Gospels

The use of *ekklēsia* does not appear equally throughout the New Testament writings. Of the 112 times it is used, ninety per cent are found in the letters of Paul, the Acts and the Book of the Revelation. Ten books do not contain the word at all—Mark, Luke, John, II Timothy, Titus, I and II Peter, I and II John and Jude—though this does not mean that the concept of the church does not occur in these writings as well.

Matthew is the only gospel to refer explicitly to the *ekklēsia* (16:18; 18:15–17). In the first of these references Jesus, in response to Peter's confession of faith in His Messiahship, declares that the apostle is the rock on which He will build His church. Here the church is spoken of in the future sense of the renewed people of God which will come into existence as a result of the redemption to be accomplished by Jesus. The second reference lays down a basic pattern for interpersonal relations and discipline within the nascent church, although the original context probably refers to a synagogue setting.

But these two passages in the first gospel do not exhaust the teaching of Jesus concerning the church. As the Son of Man, Jesus in His ministry searches out the people of God, whom He gathers to Himself and instructs concerning the impending kingdom of God. He does not limit His ministry to the larger multitude but rather calls together a small band of disciples, selects twelve to serve as leaders, and designates these as His family (Mark 3:33–34). It is to this 'little flock' (Luke 12:32; Matt. 26:31; John 10:1–18) that His Father will give the kingdom. To signify this new community of the Messiah, Jesus uses the image of the temple (Mark 13:2; 14:58). The new temple which He will build is 'the community of those who believe in Him who is the agent by whom God manifested His presence among men'.[1] At the foundation of the new temple is His atoning death and resurrection from the dead. Thus He leaves His disciples with a memorial act of communion, the Last Supper, to remind them of this fact, and a mission to preach the gospel in the whole world (Mark 13:10; Matt. 28:19–20).

The Church in Acts

The new (better, renewed) people of God concerning which our Lord spoke became a reality through the resurrection of Jesus and the coming of the promised Holy Spirit. In its original form, it was composed of a group of Jesus' former disciples plus those who responded to the early apostolic preaching in Jerusalem. At first, the infant church had the character of simply another sect within Judaism, albeit one which was distinguished from the others by the belief that

3

Jesus was the Messiah and that the forgiveness of sins and the dawn of the messianic age had come through Him. But their use of the term *ekklēsia* (Acts 5:11; 8:1,3) rather than *synagōgē* ('synagogue') for the reality represented by their community contained in it the seed of their ultimate divergence from national Israel, for in this was the claim not merely to be a local assembly of the people of God but rather to be *the* people of God and heirs of all the promises of God.[2]

As the gospel spread from Jerusalem to other parts of Palestine and Syria, and then to other provinces of the Empire, *ekklēsia* takes on two distinguishable but closely related meanings. It is used in the sense of an individual, local Christian congregation (Acts 11:26; 13:1; 14:27; 15:3; 18:22; 20:17) or of a number of such local congregations (15:41; 16:5). And, secondly, it is used in a broader sense of the whole church as far as it then existed in Judea, Galilee and Samaria (9:31, note the use of the singular). Reference to Acts 20:28 is illuminating. In context, Paul is speaking of the church in Ephesus and the responsibility of the elders (overseers) to feed the church of God (var. 'of the Lord') over which they had been given leadership, but the qualifying clause 'which He obtained with His own blood' makes it clear that more than simply the local congregation in Ephesus is in view. The idea suggested is that the church in Ephesus (and, by extension, any local congregation) is the local manifestation of *the* (universal) church of God. It is not that the church is divided up into churches, or is it that individual churches when added together as a group equal the church; rather, the church of God *in its entirety* is to be found wherever there is a group of disciples of Christ meeting together in a given locality.[3] Thus the distinction often made between the local church and the universal church is only an apparent one: each local congregation of believers, according to the New Testament, is, in fact, a microcosm of the whole church.

The Church in the Letters of Paul

This idea of each local congregation as a concrete manifestation of *the* church in a particular place is fundamental to the thought of Paul. When he writes to 'the church of God which is at Corinth' (I Cor. 1:2) or elsewhere, he does not conceive of the local community of believers in isolation from the whole body of Christians. He makes this clear in the passage just quoted by adding the words, 'to those sanctified in Christ Jesus, called to be saints together with all those who in every place call on the name of our Lord Jesus Christ, both their Lord and ours'. Therefore, Paul never speaks of 'the Corinthian church' or the like, for this usage would tend to deny the basic truth of the unity of the church and to lead toward the fragmentation of the Christian community. God's church does not belong to the people living in an individual place but rather to God and His Christ. I Thessalonians 1:1 might seem to be an exception to this general rule, but it is not. 'The church of the Thessalonians' merely indicates the locality of the church's manifestation, and the phrase 'in God the Father and the Lord Jesus Christ' makes it clear that more than simply a local congregation is in mind.

Even when Paul uses the plural of *ekklēsia* (I Thess. 2:14; Gal. 1:22; I Cor. 16:1; II Cor. 8:1; Rom. 16:16; etc.) he does not deny this basic truth. The use of the plural indicates the plurality of places where the church exists as a result of the spread of the gospel over a variety of geographical locations rather than a plurality of churches. In spite of its dispersion throughout the world, the church of God is one. The same holds true for Paul's use of the term *ekklēsia* to indicate the gathering together of the local Christian community for worship and mutual edification (I Cor. 11:18; 14:19, 23, 28, 34). Here too Paul's eye is upon the whole people of God: each gathering together of each group of Christians in a given locality for the purpose of worship embodies, at least in embryo, *the* church.

Perhaps Paul's most exalted concept of the Christian community is as the body of Christ, 'a phrase which connotes the many-faceted relations between Jesus Christ and those who belong to Him, their relations to Him as members . . ., and their relations to one another in Him. . . .'[4] The fundamental ideas embraced in this expression include the identification of believers with Christ and with one another. It is significant that Paul speaks of 'the body of Christ' and not 'the body of Christians', for the church 'depends for its existence and its unity upon the steadfast purposes of Christ rather than on the variable enthusiasms of Christians'.[5]

In I Corinthians 12:12–27, Paul speaks of the common life of believers in terms of the interdependent functioning of various parts of the human body. The body is a perfect unity; it is made up of many parts which are all necessary to the health and normal functioning of the whole. So it is with Christ's body, the church: each member has its part to play. Similarly, in Romans 12:3–8, Paul speaks of the mutual gifts and responsibilities of Christians in comparison to the diversity of functions performed by the different parts of the body. The context in the first passage is the gathering together for worship and ministry to one another, while the context of the second is more general; but the emphasis of both is on the principle of 'unity in diversity'. There is and can be only one body of Christ, since there is only one Christ (I Cor. 1:13; 10:16–17; 12:12). But each individual Christian has his role to play within that one body, and no one else can take his place. Therefore, no one should despise the contribution any member has to make in the life of the church, nor should any member think that the function he has in the body is too unimportant to be of any real value.

Paul develops the concept of the church as the body of Christ considerably in Ephesians and Colossians (Eph. 1:23; 4:12–16; 5:27–33; Col. 1:18; 2:19). In I Corinthians 12 Paul speaks of the 'head' as one of many parts of the body, along with the foot, hand, eye, ear, and the like (v. 21). His emphasis is upon the relation of the individual members to one another, and the image of the head represents one of the members of the church. In Ephesians and Colossians, however, Paul focuses on the relation of the church as the body of Christ to Christ, its Head. Here it is impossible to think of an ordinary church member being compared to the head or a part of the head of the body, for Christ is the Head. In addition, the image of the church as Christ's body now transcends mere metaphor and becomes a more realistic expression of 'the vital bond which unites the life of the people of Christ with his own risen life'.[6] The emphasis is upon the sovereignty of Christ as the risen and exalted Lord over the church, His body, and the absolute dependence of the church upon Him for its existence and growth. As the Creator finds fulfilment in His creation, so Christ is seen by the apostle as finding fulfilment in the new creation of His body, the church (Eph. 1:22–23). This body is not yet complete. It is growing and expanding, and its ultimate goal is the very fulness of God Himself (Eph. 3:17–19; 4:13). As the Head of the body, Christ rules over it, loves it, nourishes it, sanctifies it, and saves it. Through relationship to the Head, the church is filled with the glory of God (as the Tabernacle and Temple before it). The church belongs to Christ not only by virtue of who He is but because of what He has done: He gave Himself up for the church in death, as her Saviour, that the fulness of salvation might be manifest in the church. The church is the body *of Christ*; it is His own possession. The church is not autonomous, it does not exist for its own sake. Rather, it belongs to Him and exists for His sake. Christ is the One in whom the church exists (Eph. 2:21, 22), the One from whom its spiritual nourishment is derived (Eph. 4:16) and the goal toward which it moves and in whom it finds its significance (Eph. 4:15).

Images of the Church

In addition to the use of the word *ekklēsia*, a large variety of expressions and images are used by the New Testament writers to convey the idea of the church. Several of these have been mentioned already, namely, the people of God, the new temple and the body of Christ. In describing the church as *the people of God*, there is a close connection between the Old Testament and the New Testament people of God, as we have already seen indicated by the very choice of the word *ekklēsia*. In this regard a very important passage is I Peter 2:9, 'You are a chosen race, a royal priesthood, a holy nation, God's own people, that you may declare the wonderful deeds of Him who called you out of darkness into His marvellous light. Once you were no people but now you are God's people; once you had not received mercy but now you have received mercy'. Here the apostle underlines an essential continuity between the heirs of the Old Covenant and the Heirs of the New by applying four Old Testament titles of Israel to the church (see Exod. 19:5–6; Isa. 43:20–21; 44:8) and adding the phrase 'no people' from the prophecy of Hosea as an elaboration of the phrase, 'who called you out of darkness into . . . light'. True, there is a newness to the church, as verse 10 suggests; but it is new in form rather than in essence, for there can be only one people of God.

Related to the concept of the church as the people of God are such characteristic New Testament terms as saints, the sanctified, the elect, and the righteous. Each of the expressions finds its roots in the Old Testament and is originally applied to Israel. The New Testament, however, pours new meaning into the terms. *Saints* (*hagioi*) is a term applied by the New Testament to the whole people of God rather than to a select group within the church (that is, those whose lives are uniquely exemplary or who have an especially close relationship with God). The accent is not upon the moral quality of the lives of those so designated—though 'saints' are constantly exhorted by Paul and others to live up to the standards implied by their name—but rather upon the action of God. Saints are those who have been called and set apart by God to be a unique people, a people dedicated to the worship and service of God. It is God who takes the initiative in the relationship; He is the one who creates a people for Himself. Further, the use of the term 'saints' for Christian believers lays stress upon the work of the Holy Spirit (*pneuma hagion*) in the community, for saints are those who have received the gift of the Holy Spirit and in whose lives God is actively at work. Those who are 'called to be saints' are those who have been 'sanctified in Christ Jesus' (I Cor. 1:2). Thus there is a close link between the title 'saints' and the concept of sanctification, as, indeed, the two words are closely related in Greek. Here again the emphasis is not upon the moral quality of the lives of those who are sanctified but upon the sovereign action of God, Father, Son and Holy Spirit, though those who are designated 'sanctified' are called upon to live up to their high calling. Closely related are the titles *the elect* or chosen (*eklektoi*); cf. *eklegomai*, choose) and *the righteous* (*dikaioi*). The former again emphasizes the action of God rather than man in the plan of salvation: it is God who calls into being the community of the new covenant. The latter expression describes the church as made up of those whom God has 'justified' or declared to be righteous in His sight on account of the atoning sacrifice of His Son (Rom. 3:21–31). And here also the term comes directly out of the pages of the Old Testament, though the thrust given it in the New Testament adds a new dimension.

From the standpoint of man's response to God's action in Christ, the church is viewed as being made up of *believers*. In Christ, God chooses men and women to become saints, to be sanctified, and pronounces them righteous. Responding to God's call, men and women commit themselves to Him in faith (trust). Those who believe in God through Jesus Christ constitute His church. Thus the church is the company of the believers or the faithful (*pisteuontes*, cf. adjective *pistos* faithful, which is applied to God, Christ and believers). Closely related is the idea of discipleship. Those who respond to God's call become *disciples* (*mathētai*), 'those who follow' (*akolouthentes*) Christ.

The picture of the church as a *temple* or building calls forth a huge complex of images. Paul speaks of the local expression of the church (I Cor. 3:16–17), the body of individual Christians (I Cor. 6:19–20) and the whole church (Eph. 2:21, etc.; cf. Rev. 21) under this figure. The church is God's temple (*naos*) by virtue of the presence of the Triune God in its midst. The temple of God is made up of living stones (individual believers) (I Pet. 2:5; Eph. 2:22) and built upon the foundation of Christ (I Cor. 3:11) and His apostles and prophets (Eph. 2:20). Jesus is not only its Head; He is its chief cornerstone (I Pet. 2:7; Eph. 2:20). In an extension of

9

the image, believers are described as royal and holy priests in God's temple (I Pet. 2:5, 9) whose duty it is to offer up spiritual sacrifices to God (see Rom. 12:1; 15:27; II Cor. 9:12; Phil. 2:17, 25, 30).

Another capital image of the church in the New Testament is as a *family* or household, God's family. As Israel of old was frequently referred to as God's house, so in the New Testament the church is described in the same manner (Acts 2:36; Heb. 3:2–6; I Pet. 4:17; I Tim. 3:15). God is the Head and Ruler of the household, and also the One who dwells therein. To Him the entire household is related in love, obedience, dependence and stewardship. But God is no oriental despot: He is a loving Father to those who are members of His household. Therefore, those who have been called into His family are designated *sons* of God (Rom. 9:26; II Cor. 6:16–18; Heb. 2:10). The proof of their sonship is found in their receipt of the Holy Spirit whom God has sent and who enables sons of God to pray naturally, 'Abba, Father' (Gal. 4:4–6; Rom. 8:14–17). Those who have been called into God's family are also designated *brothers* (I Cor. 6:5; I Pet. 2:7; 5:9; I John 3:10–17; etc.). Within this spiritual brotherhood there is a wide variety of people from all social classes (I Cor. 1:26–27), all one in Christ (Gal. 3:28), united by a common experience of the love of God and a calling to manifest this love to one another (I John 3:10–11).

The church is often portrayed in terms of those who have responded to the call of God in Christ having enlisted in special service. A variety of terms is employed: stewards, ministers, witnesses, confessors, ambassadors, soldiers, friends, slaves and servants. Of these, the two most frequently used are the last two, carrying with them the most menial connotations. As *slaves* (*douloi*) of God/Christ, Christians are reminded that they are not their own masters but rather they belong to God both by creation and redemption (I Cor. 6:19–20). Therefore, in all their activities their ultimate obligation is to serve and please God rather than men or their own wishes and desires (I Thess. 1:9; Rom. 6:18, 22).

But the Master they serve is one who is both master and slave (Phil. 2:5–7), and in His taking the lowly place of a slave He provides a model for those who profess allegiance to Him to follow (Mark 10:44–45; II Cor. 4:5; Gal. 5:13). As *servants* (*diakonoi*) of God/Christ, believers again are reminded of their Master-Example, the One who is worthy of service yet who stoops to serve His church (John 13:3–16). With this in mind they engage in their varied form of service to one another with joy.

A full range of agricultural images is used to depict the church's dependence upon God. The church is God's *field* or farm (I Cor. 3:5–9). It is compared to a *vine* (John 15:1–6) and to an *olive tree* (Rom. 11:16–24). The image of the *first fruits* is used to picture the life of the church between the early harvest (the resurrection of Christ) and its full reaping (the Parousia) (Rom. 16:5; I Cor. 15:20; etc.). The most pervasive agricultural analogy, however, is that of the church as God's *flock*; once again we have an image with deep roots in the Old Testament. Jesus Christ is the 'great shepherd of the sheep' (Heb. 13:20) who leads, knows, cares for, protects, feeds, and gives His life for them (John 10:1–16). And He is the One who instructs His apostles and elders to care for the sheep in a similar manner (John 21:16; I Pet. 5:2). But Jesus is not only the Shepherd; He is also the Lamb (John 1:29, 36; Acts 8:32; I Pet. 1:19; Rev., 27 times). By giving His life as the Lamb, Jesus becomes qualified to be the Shepherd of the sheep; and so His sacrificial death provides an example for the care which his servants as under-shepherds should give to His flock, the church (John 21; Acts 20:28; I Pet. 5:2–4). More than this, His sacrifice becomes the model for all the sheep of His flock to follow (Rom. 8:35–39; I Pet. 2:21–25; Rev. 7:14–17).

A final image which may be noted—and there are many, many others which space will not allow to be mentioned— is the church as the *bride* of Christ. Once again the background is the Old Testament, which visualized Israel as the chosen bride of Yahweh in spite of her repeated unfaithfulness (Jer. 2:1; Ezek. 16:23; Hos. 3:1–3). In the New Testament Jesus is pictured as the bridegroom and His coming as a wedding feast (Matt. 9:15; 22:10; 25:1–13). Paul therefore speaks of having betrothed the church at Corinth to Christ 'as a pure bride to her one husband' (II Cor. 11:2). Christ as the ideal husband gives Himself in an act of total love for her salvation; the church, on her part, responds in reverence and obedience (Eph. 5:21–31). The final book of the Bible portrays the bride of the Lamb as having made herself ready by a life of faithful obedience to meet her Bridegroom on that most important Day (Rev. 19:7–9) and, under a mixed image of bride and city, as the final dwelling of God with men (21:2–27).

Conclusion

The above outline of the New Testament concept of the church is simply that—an outline. It is by no means exhaustive. Nor is it intended to give *the* doctrine of the church contained in the New Testament. For as Paul Minear writes, 'The New Testament idea of the church is not so much a technical doctrine as a gallery of pictures'.[7] Perhaps one of the reasons that there has been so much controversy among Christians concerning the doctrine of the church and the nature of its organization lies in the failure to observe this simple fact. The New Testament does not contain a totally developed and wholly consistent doctrine of church truth of the sort that might be expected in a textbook of Christian doctrine of the traditional style.

'The church is thought of as a profoundly theocentric reality, whose origins and destiny rest in the powerful initiative of God and whose life is comprised by God's call and man's response. It is a Christocentric community because Christ's work qualifies to existence of the community at every point. . . . The church is a charismatic reality, for the Holy Spirit knits together its life, and the gifts of the Spirit empower its work and determine its duties. The coherence of men in this community is characterized by the recognition of such gift-demands as love and mercy, obedience and freedom, humility and courage, holiness and sin-bearing, mutual suffering and mutual joy. There is participation, at a deep level, in common work, in daily tasks, and in an embassy to the world, wherein all members are summoned to share in worshipping and witnessing, in reconciling service and in vicarious suffering. The church is a new creation, a growing organization, a bearer of promise for the whole creation.... God's judgment begins with this household, but his presence in this household is the earnest and first fruit of final judgment and redemption of all things. The warfare between God and Satan cuts through the life of this community, where every choice registers a divided loyalty, yet it remains God's chosen instrument of action in the world, his love for the church being the sign and channel of his love for the world. Integral to its growing in the fulness of God's glory is the oneness and wholeness of the church. This oneness is enriched rather than destroyed by the diversities of the many gifts; the freedom of the many members; the scattered location of the many congregations; the gathering of men from many races, tongues, tribes, and people; and the inclusion at one table men from all generations.'[8]

NOTES

1 Ph.-H. Menoud, 'Church' *Vocabulary of the Bible* ed. J. J. von Allmen (E.T. 1958), p. 52

2 R. H. Fuller, 'Church, Assembly' *A Theological Word Book of the Bible* ed. A. Richardson (1950), p. 47

3 Cf. K. L. Schmidt, in *Theological Dictionary of the New Testament* 3 ed. G. Kittel (E.T. 1965), pp. 505–506

4 P. S. Minear, 'Christ, Body of' *Interpreter's Dictionary of the Bible* 1 ed. G. Buttrick *et al.* (1962), p. 571

5 T. W. Manson, 'Romans' *Peake's Commentary on the Bible* rev. ed. H. H. Rowley and M. Black (1962), p. 931

6 F. F. Bruce, 'The Epistles of Paul' *Peake's Commentary* p. 930

7 'Church, Idea of' *IDB* 1, p. 617

8 *Ibid.* pp. 616–617

2

Baptism and the Lord's Supper

MURRAY J. HARRIS

Among the means of grace available to the Christian believer, the sacraments of baptism and the Lord's Supper have an important place. A sacrament or ordinance is a symbolic rite, instituted by Christ for perpetual observance, which dramatizes the central truths of the Christian faith and strengthens the faith of the Christian.

It has been well said that whenever the Word of God is proclaimed, the gospel is presented to eargate; but whenever a believer is baptized or the Lord's Supper is celebrated, the gospel is presented to eyegate. So the submersion of the Christian in water is an acted parable of the death and burial of Christ, while his emergence from the water graphically dramatizes Christ's rising from death and entrance into new life (Rom. 6:4; Col. 2:12). Again, the breaking and eating of the loaf and the pouring and drinking of the wine at Communion vividly portray Christ's voluntary surrender of Himself to death and the Christian's sharing in the benefits of His propitiatory sacrifice.

But not only are these two sacraments dramatic signs; they are effective symbols. God's love and grace are poured into our hearts through the Holy Spirit when we obey Christ in baptism and feed on Him at Communion.

Institution by Christ

Communion is called the '*Lord's* Supper', not only because His death and life are recalled and appropriated at each celebration, but also because He Himself directed its observance as a matter of perpetual and universal obligation (I Cor. 11:24 'Do this in remembrance of Me').

14

It is in Matt. 28:16–20 that we find the dominical authority for baptism as an ordinance of the Christian church. Two of the principal means to be employed by Christ's followers in bringing all nations under Christian discipleship are baptism in the Triune Name and direction in the observance of the commands of Jesus. Behind the command of the risen Jesus to baptize lay His own submission to a baptism of water at the Jordan and to a baptism of blood at Calvary.

Relation of Baptism and the Lord's Supper

We have seen that these two rites have this in common: they form a non-verbal communication of the gospel, visibly portraying the realities of the faith. But whereas baptism is an individual rite administered in the presence of witnesses, the Lord's Supper involves the corporate participation of the members of the Body of Christ. The local church celebrates holy Communion, the individual Christian is baptized. Secondly, while the Lord's Supper should be regularly celebrated, baptism is a once-for-all experience. The death of Christ was a single, unrepeatable act involving all men (II Cor. 5:14f). By undergoing baptism on one definite occasion, each Christian indicates that Christ's one baptism for all men has become personally effective. Baptism has to do with initiation into the Faith and entry into a church, communion with continuance in faith and renewal in devotion.

Baptism

Terminology (Mode of Baptism)

Traditionally in the Christian Church baptism has been administered in one of three ways: sprinkling water on the head (aspersion); pouring water over the head and body (affusion or infusion); immersing the candidate in water (submersion).

In the New Testament, as in the Greek Old Testament, the verb *baptō* means 'dip' or 'immerse' (for example, Exod.

15

12:22; Job 9:31; Luke 16:24; John 13:26). Its intensive or iterative form *baptizō* (which gives us the English word 'baptize') regularly means 'immerse' (or 'submerge'), but passages such as Luke 11:38, Acts 1:5 (cf. 2:4) or I Corinthians 10:2 show that the verb does not necessarily imply immersion or a 'deluging' and can, on occasion, refer to ceremonial washing, whether involving bathing, sprinkling or pouring. But it remains true to say that *baptizō* normally refers to immersion beneath water. Thus in Greek literature the term was used in a literal sense of the sinking of ships or metaphorically of a person's being inundated or overwhelmed with questions.

Antecedents

1. *Proselyte Baptism.* The evidence for Jewish proselyte baptism early in the first century A.D. is slender, but it seems sufficient to establish that before John's baptism or the institution of Christian baptism a rite was being administered on non-Jews which marked their admission into the body of the chosen people and their new status under God's protection and law as 'sons of the covenant'.

2. *John's Baptism.* Like proselyte baptism, John's baptism was administered only once, took place in flowing water, and was by immersion. Yet John was distinctive in his insistence on the need for repentance in readiness for the coming day of wrath and the advent of the Messiah (Matt. 3:1–3, 7f, 11), his demand that Jews should submit to his baptism (Acts 13:24, and note John 1:25), and his own administration of the rite (proselytes baptized themselves in the presence of three rabbis who constituted a court)—hence his title 'John the Baptizer'.

3. *The Baptism of Jesus.* It has been well observed that in the voice from heaven there is found both the coronation formula of the Messianic King of Israel ('Thou art My beloved Son' cf. Ps. 2:7) and the ordination formula of the Servant of Yahweh ('. . . with Whom I am well pleased'; cf. Isa. 42:1). Moreover, Jesus would have discerned in this divine word His Father's appointment of Him as the new Isaac destined to be

offered up (see Rom. 8:32, and note the conjunction of *agapētos* and *huios*, 'beloved son' in Gen. 22:2, 12, 16, LXX).

So significant to Jesus was His baptism by John that He could subsequently refer to His own decease in Jerusalem as a baptism, as submersion in the waters of death (Mark 10:38; Luke 12:50). His 'baptism of repentance' in the Jordan as representative Man foreshadowed His baptism of blood at Calvary as a Substitute for sinful man (cf. I John 5:6). In one case He confessed national guilt, identifying Himself with the sins of the nation; in the other, He bore universal guilt, suffering for the sins of the world.

4. *The Baptism of Jesus' Disciples.* As a preparatory rite, the baptism administered by the disciples of Jesus (John 3:22, 26; 4:1f) was undoubtedly more akin to John's baptism than to Christian baptism since the latter lacked its *raison d'être* until the death and resurrection of Christ. Perhaps just as Jesus continued John's preaching (Matt. 4:17; cf. 3:1f), so Jesus' disciples may have continued John's baptism, the one difference being that those who were baptized thus identified themselves as followers of the Messiah.

Candidates and their Preparation

Some of the more important arguments in favour of the practice of believers' (note, not adult) baptism and against the practice of infant baptism (paedobaptism) may be summarily stated:

(a) The New Testament contains no explicit instance of infant baptism. References to household baptisms (Acts 16:14f, 32–34; 18:8; I Cor. 1:14, 16) seem to exclude children, since the context always implies the intelligent and personal response of members of the household to a proclaimed message.

(b) In the New Testament baptism followed a personal confession of Christ (Rom. 10:9f; I Tim. 6:12 and perhaps I Pet. 3:21). One came to baptism, was not brought to baptism. And the New Testament knows nothing of vicarious faith.

(c) Infant baptism divides a single New Testament rite into

two separate ceremonies—baptism and (subsequently) confirmation.

(d) It is not at all certain that the New Testament (for example in Col. 2:11f) regards Christian baptism as the New Covenant substitute for circumcision (which was performed on Jewish male children on the eighth day after birth). Circumcision itself no more made a person Jewish than baptism makes a person a Christian. Behind circumcision was natural birth, behind baptism is the 'new birth'.

(e) The paedobaptist appeal to I Corinthians 7:14 sometimes overlooks the fact that children are 'holy' *before* baptism and because of their relation to a Christian parent or to Christian parents, not because of baptism.

(f) The logical corollary of paedobaptism would seem to be infant participation in the Lord's Supper.

Probably baptismal candidates were prepared for baptism by being given specific instruction about Christian belief and conduct and possibly by a pre-baptismal fast (cf. Acts 9:9, 18f). There are traces in New Testament epistles of stylized Christian instruction (cf. Heb. 6:2) which would have been given to candidates for baptism or to recently baptized converts: (a) doctrinal catechesis, involving credal confessions (for example, I Tim. 3:16); and (b) ethical catechesis, involving injunctions to 'put off' the old nature, to practise Christian submission, to 'watch and pray', and to stand firm in the faith and resist the devil (for example I Pet. 2:11–3:7; 5:8f).

The Baptismal Formula and the Baptizer

It is a remarkable fact that although the risen Christ enjoined His disciples to baptize 'in the name of the Father and of the Son and of the Holy Spirit' (Matt. 28:19), the New Testament records no case of baptism in the Triune Name— only of baptism 'into the name of the Lord Jesus' (Acts 8:16; 19:5) or 'in the name of Jesus Christ' (Acts 2:38; 10:48).

The difficulty may be explained by the observation that baptism in the name of one Person of the Trinity amounts to baptism in the name of the Trinity, or (better) that the

Lucan formulas, abbreviated forms of the Matthean, may not indicate the precise words used in Christian baptisms—actually the Trinitarian formula—but rather may point to the theological significance of baptism. In baptism there is a transference of the rights of possession ('into the name', *eis to onoma*, Acts 8:16; 19:5) and an invocation of the name of Christ by the candidate or the pronouncing of Christ's name by the baptizer ('in the name', *epi tō onomati*, Acts 2:38, *en tō onomati*, Acts 10:48; cf. 22:16).

The privilege of administering baptism did not belong, it seems, to any one group within a church. Philip, the deacon-evangelist, baptized the Ethiopian chamberlain (Acts 8:38) and probably the Samaritans (Acts 8:12f), while Paul, the founder of the Corinthian church, baptized Crispus, Gaius and the household of Stephanas (I Cor. 1:14–17). Ananias, 'a certain disciple', probably baptized Saul (Acts 9:10, 18; 22:16) and 'the brethren from Joppa' may have baptized Cornelius and his company, in obedience to Peter's command (Acts 10:23, 47f).

Baptism, Faith, and the Gift of the Spirit

Although there is disagreement within Christendom over the mode and proper recipients of baptism, almost all agree that faith and baptism belong together, however their relation be expressed. Exceptionally, faith without baptism was possible (for example, the repentant robber in Luke 23:42f) and on occasion baptism was not accompanied by faith (for example, Simon Magus in Acts 8:9–24). But normally in New Testament times, the profession of faith in Christ was promptly—sometimes immediately (Acts 16:25–34)—followed by baptism in obedience to Christ. An unbaptized Christian is an anomaly in the New Testament and has been likened to 'a testator who has made a will but has not signed it' (A. Plummer). Like good deeds, which do not make a person a Christian but are a Christian obligation (Titus 2:14), baptism is a proof of faith, an evidence of submission to the lordship of Christ. Just as 'faith without works is dead' (Jas. 2:26),

19

faith without the good work of baptism is incomplete (cf. Jas. 2:22).

Thus Paul can say that both belief with the heart and confession with the lips (at baptism) are the prerequisite of salvation (Rom. 10:9f) and Peter can refer to baptism (regarded as the expression of faith) as a means by which salvation comes (I Pet. 3:21; Acts 2:38; cf. 22:16 and note John 3:5, 'born of water', and Heb. 10:22. Mark 16:16 is almost certainly non-canonical). As its natural expression faith demands baptism. For its validity baptism demands faith. Two dangers are to be avoided—faith without baptism and baptism without faith.

The ordinance of baptism, considered by itself, no more imparts the Holy Spirit than it creates faith (cf. Acts 8:14–16; 10:44–48). Yet the receipt of the Spirit is often closely associated with water-baptism (John 3:5; Acts 2:28; 9:17f; I Cor. 6:11; Titus 3:5). Christian baptism in water may be distinguished from Spirit baptism (Matt. 3:11; John 1:33; Acts 1:5) (although in the case of Jesus Spirit baptism and water baptism were apparently united, Matt. 3:16). By the baptism of the Spirit is meant the believer's incorporation into the one Body of Christ (I Cor. 12:13; cf. Eph. 4:4), and his being sealed by the Spirit, that is, his receipt of the Spirit as the pledge of inheritance (Rom. 8:9, 11; II Cor. 1:22; 5:5; Eph. 1:13f; 4:30). By water baptism there takes place the individual believer's incorporation into some visible Christian fellowship, his public admission into the Spirit-baptized community. Yet Gal. 3:27f demonstrates the intimate connection between the outward and visible sign (immersion in water) and the inward and spiritual grace (the baptism of the Spirit).

Significance of Baptism

As he submits to baptism in obedience to Christ's command, the believer gives outward evidence, by an oral and public confession, of his inward belief in Jesus Christ as the Son of God and his intent to show lifelong devotion and loyalty to his Master with whom he has died, been buried and raised (Rom. 6:1–11).

As the natural expression of faith, baptism marks the believer's entry into the fellowship of a local church and signifies his antecedent incorporation into the Church of Christ. Baptism is an outward sign of prior inward cleansing (I Pet. 3:21). Only in this sense can baptism be called 'the sacrament of justification by faith'.

Moreover baptism is a seal which confirms God's grace and stimulates our faith. In baptism God the Father acknowledges His present possession of us and pledges His future care for us as His adopted sons (cf. Matt. 3:17) who walk in newness of life (Rom. 6:4; Eph. 2:5f), and we respond by faith to that divine reassurance and pledge, owning His exclusive rights over us. Baptism looks back to God's grace and forward to His faithfulness, back to our death to sin and forward to our risen and then resurrection life with Christ.

The Lord's Supper

Terminology

This sacrament is commonly described by four expressions.

1. *The Breaking of Bread*. 'Breaking bread', a common New Testament phrase (Acts 2:46; 20:7, 11; 27:35; I Cor. 10:16; 11:23f) and compare 'the breaking of the loaf' in Luke 24:35; Acts 2:42, was a technical expression for the Jewish custom of pronouncing the blessing and breaking and distributing the bread at the beginning of a meal. But it came to refer to the fellowship meal or informal supper of shared food, during which Christians formally celebrated the Lord's Supper. It included both the Agape (love-feast) and the Eucharist (Acts 20:7, 11), both social and sacramental aspects.

2. *The Lord's Supper*.   Whether *kuriakon deipnon* (I Cor. 11:20; 10:21; Rev. 19:9) means 'the (Last) Supper of the Lord' (cf. John 13:2–4; 21:20), or, as is more probable, 'the Lord's Supper', the reference is to a meal at which the Lord presided.

3. *Communion*.   In I Corinthians 10:16 Paul speaks of the cup

of blessing and the broken bread as signifying a 'communion' (Greek, *koinōnia*; Latin *communio*) or participation in the blood and body of Christ, in the benefits of His death.

4. *The Eucharist.* Since Christ gave thanks (Greek, *eucharistēsas*) for the bread (Luke 22:19; I Cor. 11:23f) and the cup (Matt. 26:27; Mark 14:23) at the Last Supper and the offering of thanks (Greek, *eucharistia*) is an integral part of Communion (I Cor. 10:16; cf. 14:16), the term Eucharist is often used to designate the Lord's Supper.

The Last Supper

The Last Supper of the Lord was not the first Lord's Supper but rather its promise. The Lord's Supper was the successor of the Last Supper and of all the fellowship meals Jesus shared with His disciples during His ministry (see Matt. 11:19; Luke 15:2) and after His resurrection (Luke 24:30–43; John 21:9–14; Acts 10:41). In the record of the Synoptic gospels the Last Supper seems to be simply a regular celebration of the Passover (Greek, *pascha*) (Mark 14:12–16; Luke 22:15f), but the fourth gospel has the crucifixion itself occurring as the paschal lambs were being slain during the Day of Preparation, the Last Supper being held on the night before the Passover (John 13:1f; 18:28; 19:14, 31, 42).

Those who seek to harmonize the apparent discrepancies between the Synoptic and Johannine accounts often appeal to the use in heterodox Judaism of a calendar different from that of official Jewry, suggesting that the Synoptics followed a Pharisaic dating of the Passover and John a Sadducean dating. Whatever be the solution to this complex problem it is fair to claim that Passover ideas suffused the celebration of the Last Supper and therefore supply the key to the proper interpretation of the Lord's Supper which thus becomes the Christian Passover feast. So Paul can identify Christ as the paschal Lamb (I Cor. 5:7).

The Words of Institution

The New Testament contains four accounts of the institution

of this memorial feast (Matt. 26:26–29; Mark 14:22–25; Luke 22:15–20; I Cor. 11:23–26; cf. 10:16) and their comparison forms an illuminating study.

'This is My body (which is given for you)' means 'This broken bread I hold in My hands stands for or signifies My physical body which is about to be broken for you in death'. For parallel uses of this explanatory 'is' (which implies not identity but representation), see Matt. 13:19–23, 37–39; Gal. 4:24f; Rev. 1:20. 'This is My blood of the covenant (which is poured out for many for the forgiveness of sins)' has the sense 'The wine in this cup represents My life's blood soon to be voluntarily shed by Me that the new covenant may be ratified and the sins of all may be forgiven' (cf. Exod. 24:8; Isa. 42:6; 53:12; Jer. 31:31, 34). The Pauline form (I Cor. 11:25), 'This cup is the new covenant in My blood', may be paraphrased 'This cup of wine symbolizes the new relationship between God and man established at the price of My covenant blood'. Note that these words of administration (not consecration) were spoken to His disciples, not to the elements. When Jesus added 'Truly, I say to you, I shall not drink again of the fruit of the vine until that day when I drink it new in the kingdom of God' (Mark 14:25), He may have expressed His solemn resolve to refrain from sharing with His disciples the fourth cup of wine in the paschal meal; certainly He expressed His determination to drink the cup of suffering by which the perfect fellowship of the kingdom would be made possible.

Participants
The guests invited to the Lord's table (I Cor. 10:21) include all His professed followers. In New Testament times, this would mean all those who had been baptized (cf. Matt. 28:19f; Acts 2:41f) since the profession of faith was promptly followed by baptism. Yet some invited guests forfeit their right of attendance, owing to their immoral conduct (I Cor. 5:1–13), their disobedience to the commands of Christ or His apostles (II Thess. 3:6, 14f), or an adherence to doctrinal error, that causes division (Rom. 16:17; Titus 3:10f; II John 9–11).

While no guest is inherently worthy to attend, each is to conduct himself in a manner befitting the high privilege and solemn occasion (I Cor. 11:28), lest he incur God's displeasure and remedial punishment, be it illness or death (I Cor. 11:29–32). The context of I Corinthians 11:29 would indicate that 'without discerning the body' refers to participation while in a schismatic state or harbouring an unforgiving and therefore divisive spirit, or to the failure—apparent in selfish or irreverent conduct— to recognize the corporate body or discern that the elements represent the Lord's body.

Day, Time, and Frequency

For a period, in some churches the love-feast and the Lord's Supper possibly were held daily (Acts 2:46; cf. 3:1; 6:1). Then the Supper came to be celebrated weekly 'on the first day of the week' (Acts 20:7; cf. John 20:19, 26; I Cor. 16:2), 'the Lord's Day' (Rev. 1:10). For Christians, Sunday was the day of the new creation in Christ, the day of Christ's resurrection, the day on which He had held table-fellowship with two of His disciples (Luke 24:13, 28–30) 'As often' in I Corinthians 11:25f probably implies regularity (cf. John 20:19, 26) but not frequency. The weekly Jewish sabbath (Exod. 31:12–17; Ezek. 20:12, 20) rather than the annual Passover (Exod. 13:10) provided the model for the frequency of the Christian observance of the Lord's Supper.

Originally, Jewish Christians, who continued their sabbath worship in the temple or synagogue (Acts 2:46; 3:1; 5:20f, 42), may have met after sundown on Saturday evening for Christian fellowship and to 'celebrate the festival'. But by A.D. 57 Sunday evening had become (at least in Asia Minor) the regular time of meeting, if Acts 20:7, 11 be a guide (observe that the 'morrow' after 'the first day of the week' was marked by 'daybreak', not sunset). And the practice in the Roman province of Bithnyia early in the second century was to meet 'on a certain fixed day before daybreak' (Pliny, *Epistles*, x. 96–97). The Greek word (*deipnon*) translated 'supper' need not imply an evening meal.

Procedure

Christ is present at His Supper not as an unseen Guest but as the presiding Host. But if Christ is president, who may act as celebrant? Nowhere in the Pastoral epistles—where church order is a primary concern—is it suggested that the dispensing of the elements at the Lord's table or the offering of the prayers of thanksgiving is a privilege reserved for a special group, whether presbyters or deacons. Probably an apostle, if present, would have dispensed the emblems (Acts 20:11), but the New Testament lays down no special qualification for the duty (see Acts 2:46).

Paul directs that participants who have a hymn, lesson, revelation or prophecy should speak in a disciplined fashion, one by one, and for the instruction and encouragement of all (I Cor. 14:26, 31f; cf. 14:3–5, 19), showing deference to other gifted persons (I Cor. 14:30), while listeners are to exercise discernment concerning what is said (I Cor. 14:29; cf. 12:3, 10).

Associated with the Eucharist in the apostolic age was the communal meal or love-feast (alluded to in Acts 2:42, 46; 20:7, 11; I Cor. 11:21f; Jude 12 and perhaps II Pet. 2:13), a spontaneous expression of brotherly love which was fittingly climaxed by Communion. After the Agape there may have been exchanged the 'holy kiss' of love (mentioned in Rom. 16:16; I Cor. 16:20; II Cor. 13:12; I Thess. 5:26; I Pet. 5:14) as a sign of forgiveness and reconciliation (cf. Matt. 5:23f) before sharing in the single loaf and the single cup which expressively symbolize the unity of believers in the mystical body of Christ (I Cor. 10:17). At some stage in the proceedings distribution to the needy was made out of the common fund (cf. Acts 2:44f; 4:32, 34f; 6:1).

Significance

As the Christian Passover repast, the Lord's Supper has a threefold significance—past, present and future.

1. Just as the Jewish Passover feast commemorated God's

mighty deliverance of Israel from Egyptian bondage through the death of a lamb (Exod. 12:1–13:10), so in Communion believers celebrate the emancipation of the New Israel from bondage to sin and death, a deliverance brought about by the death of the paschal Lamb of God (I Cor. 5:7). Only the first Passover was a sacrifice. Subsequent Passovers were memorials of that sacrifice and deliverance. Similarly the Lord's Supper is not a repetition of Christ's sacrificial death but a commemoration of His sacrifice by which the new covenant was established (Heb. 12:24; 13:20). Ancient Near Eastern covenants provided for the regular reiteration of the terms of the covenant to enable the vassals perpetually to recall their covenantal commitments to their master. In light of Heb. 9:26, 28; 10:10, 12, 'Do this in remembrance of Me' (I Cor. 11:24) cannot involve the 're-presentation' to God of the sacrifice of Christ. That the Supper commemorates Christ's resurrection as well as His death is shown by the early association of Sunday (not Friday) with the celebration.

What is more, in the Lord's Supper Christ's death is 'proclaimed' (I Cor. 11:26; cf. Exod. 12:26f; 13:8). This central fact of the gospel is proclaimed in action in a pictorial dramatization. The very separation of the wine from the loaf on the table suggests the violent separation of the blood from the body or flesh in a sacrificial victim. The emblematic bread is broken and the wine poured out. Believers personally partake of these elements, portraying the need for the individual appropriation of secured benefits. The proclamation involves not primarily words but actions—eating and drinking after the breaking and pouring.

2. Secondly, at every celebration of the Passover Jews were reminded that God strengthens His people for their journey (Exod. 12:8, 11) and that He providentially cares for them and sustains them during the journey. In addition, their sharing of the common meal expressed and confirmed their unity. Consequently to betray the trust symbolized by table-fellowship was to be guilty of treachery (Ps. 41:9; Luke 22:19–23).

Those who 'partake of the table' of the one Lord (1 Cor.

10:21; Eph. 4:5), who share the one loaf and the one cup, dramatize their corporate fellowship and unity in Christ (I Cor. 10:16f). An individual celebration of 'Communion' amounts to a contradiction in terms. Moreover, at this time Christians enjoy individual fellowship with the risen Christ, the Source and Sustainer of life (John 5:21, 26; 14:6; Col. 1:17; Heb. 1:3). Just as the assimilated physical elements of bread and wine contribute to physical nourishment, so the communicant gains spiritual nourishment through Christ's spiritual entry into his life. 'He who eats Me will live because of Me' (John 6:57; cf. I Cor. 10:1–4; Rev. 3:20). In union with one another, believers enjoy communion with Christ.

To the Jewish mind 'remembering' was no simple recollection of a past event; it involved the personal experience of its present consequences. To remember was to receive as well as to recall. In the Eucharist we not only recall the death of Christ but also appropriate its benefits. It is to the faith and in the heart of the believer that Christ (who is corporally in heaven) is spiritually yet really present. His is no bodily presence localized in or under the elements. The prayer of Christians at Communion is that Christ may be as real to their spiritual senses as the emblems are to their physical senses.

3. For the Jews the Passover was also a pointer to the Messiah's coming and an anticipation of the banquet to be celebrated in the Messianic Age (Isa. 25:6; 65:13; Matt. 8:11). Hence the saying of the rabbis: 'On this night they were saved, and on this night they will be saved'.

As well as being a memorial of Christ's passion and a sharing of His risen life, the Lord's Supper is a promise of His return (Luke 22:16, 18, 29f; I Cor. 11:26, 'until He comes'). Between the Exodus and the Messianic Age was the annual celebration of the Passover. Between the Cross and the second Advent is the weekly celebration of the Lord's Supper. The early Christian prayer *Marana tha* ('Our Lord, come!', I Cor. 16:22) was offered after worship in expectation of His Parousia (and possibly also before worship, in expectation of His real presence at His Supper). This accounts for the spontaneous joy which characterized each celebration of this thanksgiving festival (Acts 2:46).

Both Christian sacraments are retrospective and prospective: they look back to the single sacrifice of Christ and forward to the Christian's life of faith, back to Christ's first Advent and forward to His second Advent. When the Kingdom finally and fully comes, the sacraments will become superfluous and Christ will be present with believers in a manner not previously experienced. Commemoration is pointless when the one commemorated is personally present.

3

Leadership and Authority in the Church

WALTER L. LIEFELD

The course of biblical history, to say nothing of world history, provides innumerable examples of the crucial importance of strong, vital leadership. This is seen from such diverse circumstances as the dynamic movement of the Exodus, the chequered careers of the kings, and the dismal state reflected in Judges, relieved only by the appearance of an occasional leader.

The church of Jesus Christ needs leadership more, not less, than the people of God in Old Testament times. The church is scattered around the earth and under a commission impossible except for constant diligence in the power of the Spirit. Without a visible royal or military leader, without geographical goals by which to measure success, without civil and ceremonial laws as an external indication, of sorts, of obedience to God's commands, the church today could wallow in stagnant complacency without wise, authoritative and esteemed leadership. As Moses appointed seventy to help him, and then Joshua to succeed him, so the church must make provision of continuing leadership one of its main orders of spiritual business.

The two terms, leadership and authority, are overlapping and yet distinct. Together they indicate the orderly direction which is essential if a church is to function efficiently in obedience to the Lord. When we think of *leadership*, we probably have in mind the activity of those whom we trust and admire, who show us the way to the accomplishment of those purposes Christ has for his church. When we speak about *authority*, we refer to the right of these leaders to teach

29

and discipline a local church, to the end that it be holy and obedient to the revealed will of God. Such men must give account to God for the spiritual condition of the church. Ideally, both functions are centred, though not exclusively, in the elders of the local church. Their work is supplemented by that of the deacons, whose basic function may be generally described as *stewardship*.

Owing to our human failings, we need to guard against both a static authority and mercurial leadership. We have all observed that the more highly one views his commission under the authority of Christ, the more one may be tempted to assume an air of infallibility and to identify oneself with the authority he represents, thereby becoming intolerably authoritarian. On the other hand, one may exercise a popular leadership apart from the controls of biblical authority and thus become an undisciplined enthusiast, leading the church into division. Therefore, we must be concerned not only with the structure of church government, but also with its nature, purposes and function. Only then are we prepared to grapple with issues of biblical and contemporary urgency as they affect the life of the church.

The Structure of Church Government

As the church developed in scope and complexity, the structure of government likewise developed, although not necessarily in linear fashion, from simple to complex. The varieties of church government practised today reflect differing assessments of the biblical data. The issue is not simply between different forms of government, but between different appraisals of the biblical sources. Are we to take the practices described in Acts as normative or as mainly descriptive? Some would add a third option, that they are idealized pictures of the early church which actually reflect later church practice. This raises the question of the date and provenance of Acts. If we assume, for reasons which cannot be discussed within the limits of this article, that our choice is basically between the first two options, how are we to correlate the relatively unstructured church pictured in Acts with the more structured church of Timothy and Titus? Several approaches have been taken. 1. We may decide that it is the Epistles which are normative, providing a pattern to be followed today, with Acts only describing the development prior to the final structuring of the New Testament church. 2. We may conclude that the New Testament does not seek to impose any rigid structure. Thus we are free, for example, to have both elders and deacons (Phil. 1:2; I Tim. 3:1–13) or only elders (Acts 11:30; 14:23, which do not mention deacons). Perhaps the group mentioned in Acts 6 were not deacons (or elders), but an *ad hoc* committee which is not intended to serve as an exemplar. 3. Alternatively, we may decide to build on all such references, harmonizing where necessary, in the conviction that everything is normative and binding. 4. Another view which has been put forward is that both the Acts and the Epistles are indeed normative, but that the church now lies 'in ruins' and cannot be reproduced in its apostolic purity. 5. It has even been suggested that early church government was somewhat like that of the Dead Sea Community of Qumran: decisions were made variously by a single official, by a council, and by the entire community. This, it is claimed, might justify all ecclesiastical forms, episcopal, presbyterian, and congregational.

In finding our way through these various options, several principles must be followed. First, all the New Testament should be considered instructive, even if some parts are not held to be normative. What may be only descriptive will still provide insight as to how decisions were reached and leadership exercised. Thus, while some scriptures will not be found to be normative as to structure or method they may be normative as to spirit and principle.

Secondly, the principle of collegiality was an essential feature of New Testament leadership. In every instance where authority seems invested in an individual, such as in Acts 15 and the Epistles to Timothy and Titus, a plurality of elders is also indicated. There is no clear instance of any church being under the leadership of a single individual beyond a transitional period. In addition, the domination of any one person is decisively rejected in III John 9. (The mention of a 'messenger' (*angellos*) connected with each of the seven churches in Revelation 2 and 3 is ambiguous. Some regard this as a reference to the 'pastor' or 'bishop' in each case, but there are more probable interpretations.)[1]

A third principle is that the careful presentation of detailed qualifications for deacons and elders is not incidental but for our guidance today. Our distance from apostolic times and the lesser degree of unity and integrity in the church today must not prevent us from seeking, training and choosing elders and deacons as surely as was done by the apostles. Otherwise, we render inoperative the first chapter of Titus and the third chapter of I Timothy.

Recognition of Elders

Related to these matters is the method by which church leaders are to be chosen. Granted that it is the Holy Spirit who appoints the leaders (Acts 20:28), how is God's choice communicated to the church? Initially it was by apostolic designation (Acts 14:23). But does the passing of the apostolic generation and, some would add, the degeneration of the church, pose an insoluble problem? Some reject any action suggestive of an election. Contending that sheep do not choose a shepherd, they point out that popular figures rather than qualified men might be elected. It is affirmed, correctly, that those who ought to be recognized as elders will become known to the church by their life and service; election does not make an elder. In some circles, however, the matter is left there. Individuals are not openly and decisively recognized by the church as a whole. Consequently there is no distinct body of elders, such as is clearly implied in Acts 20:17 and Philippians 1:2.

But how can an assembly provide for the recognition of elders in a manner which avoids the dangers not only of an election but also of the self-perpetuation of elders, privately arranged, which may degenerate into favouritism and an ingrown oligarchy? One method which builds squarely on the biblical descriptions of an elder's life and work is carried out as follows. The Scriptural qualifications are written down in summary under the three heads of teaching, counselling and ruling, with an explanation of the unique requirements of each. All in the fellowship of the local church are requested to mention under each category those whom they consider to be most qualified. (A person may be mentioned under only one or two headings, if that seems appropriate.) Brief statements may be included, citing the reasons why those named are considered qualified. Those presently serving as elders are mentioned (or omitted) on the same basis as everyone else.

This provides the elders with an understanding of how the church views its present values as well as others who might be considered as additions to the eldership. At the same time, the church is reminded of the character and function of elders, and all are encouraged to seek biblical leadership. The present elders then decide who should become, or continue, as elders, using wisely and in confidence the information gathered from the church. Those whose eldership is not supported by the church should consider resigning. Those who were occasionally named, but perhaps not yet considered ready by the elders, can be encouraged on in their Christian life and service with a view to possible later recognition. This procedure can be repeated at appropriate intervals, with the elders at liberty to name new elders at any time in between.

It should be apparent that if the biblical ideal of strong, recognized church leadership is not realized, it is small virtue to have avoided error in the relatively less important method of selection. We dare not let our legitimate concern to have a spiritually appropriate method of recognition so paralyze us that we lapse into the uncertainties of an undefined elderhood or into the grip of a self-proclaimed dictatorship like that of Diotrephes. These perilous alternatives may sometimes arise from a failure to realize the importance of the *corporate* authority of elders.

The Corporate Authority of Elders
From the various descriptions of elders in the New Testament, we gather that their work can be considered

under the three overlapping categories mentioned above: teaching, counselling and ruling. Of these three functions, only counselling and teaching can be done individually (and that only in part), for no individual elder has authority to rule over other people. This function is only possible as the elders act corporately. If a decision is to be implemented by the church, and especially if this involves discipline, it is imperative that the action not be compromised by uncertainty as to the authority of those who have taken it. Decisions regarding the doctrine to be maintained and taught are also a corporate responsibility, involving the elders' authority both to teach and to rule.

Even closer to the heart of the matter is the *nature* of this authority. As we shall see, we have instructive biblical examples of the exercise of authority in the early church. We can also learn from the vocabulary employed in the New Testament. This includes words which were sometimes used in non-biblical writings in an official sense. Does their use in the New Testament, however, support an elderhood conceived of as an 'office', as in the King James translation of *episkopē* in I Timothy 3:1 (the office of a bishop)? This reflects the development of ideas concerning church government over the centuries. (One might also cite the use of the word 'ordain', to translate some twenty different Hebrew and Greek words, most of them common rather than technical in meaning.)

Actually, Scripture employs a number of words with varying secular and religious associations, among them *episkopos*, 'overseer' (cf. *episkopē* above); *presbuteros*, 'elder'; *hegeomai*, 'lead'; and *proistēmi*, 'rule'. It is not possible here to discuss the history and usage of such terminology,[2] but several observations might be made. Their variety and the fact that they were to some degree interchangeable (as in Titus 1:5, 7) indicates that no one pattern of pre-Christian government, secular or Jewish, was carried over intact into Christianity. The strongest precedent, of course, was the eldership of the Jewish synagogue. Also the meaning of a particular context is often debatable. What was the *episkopē* of

Judas (Acts 1:20)? Must it have been an 'office', or could we better call it a duty or function? Nevertheless, while we may question certain ecclesiastical interpretations of the New Testament vocabulary, the words must not be taken lightly. They do convey a weighty sense of dignity and authority.

As an example which is sometimes overlooked, we might cite the use of the word *proistēmi*, usually translated 'rule'. In the secular world it was commonly used to describe leadership of a group or party. It tended to have an activistic sense. That is to say, stress was not merely on the status of the leader but on his administrative activity. He 'stood before' as a leader moves out in front to encourage and guide the others toward their common goal. The biblical usage of the word illustrates how this was done in the local church. When Timothy was instructed that some elders should receive double honour (or 'stipend', NEB), the church was to consider especially those who ruled well, laboured in the word and taught (I Tim. 5:17). When Paul advised the Thessalonians that they were to acknowledge and esteem these leaders, these were described as working hard and admonishing the believers (I Thess. 5:12f). Such statements do not minimize authority; but they do stress the work and qualities of leadership, especially through the medium of biblical instruction. They stand as a warning against any who merely seek the honour of an office.

The relationship a leader has to the church is parallel to that which a father has in his family, as I Timothy 3:4f (in which *proestēmi* also occurs) clearly indicates. The analogy of the family, therefore, also helps us to understand the nature and function of authority in the church. Discipline and submission are essential, not only in occasional instances of correction (or excommunication) but in the way daily training is administered and accepted. It is the latter which characterized the relationship the young Jesus had with His parents (Luke 2:51). The words 'respectful in every way' (I Tim. 3:5) imply that obedience is to be more than external. It is not just order, but a healthy atmosphere of mutual esteem, which is to characterize both home and church.

In short, everything important in family relations, and indeed in human relations in general, is important in the church. Decisions are to be reached with full consideration of, and in communication with, all those involved. These decisions are to be open and unambiguous, clearly related to acknowledged goals. The lines of both authority and responsibility are to be openly understood and maintained. The church above all other associations should be concerned not simply with *what* decisions are reached, but *how* they are made.

In those instances where severe correctional discipline is needed, the goal is always the glory of God and the restoration of the offender. As in family relations, the justice of the situation and the good of all must take precedence over the emotional reaction of those involved. Feelings of anger and retribution must not control, nor must sentimentalism. The same reactions of severity or leniency which distort discipline in the home and in society can intrude into church discipline. Such Scriptures as Matthew 18:15–22; I Corinthians 5:1–13; and Acts 5:1–16 must be diligently studied and the principles followed. We also have several helpful examples in Scripture of both decision making and discipline, such as Paul's very human and yet responsible attitude to the Corinthian church and the errant brother, the response to legitimate complaints in Acts 6, and the major decision of Acts 15. With these examples we move into the territory common to authority and leadership. Thus we observe such evidences of wise leadership as the delegation of authority in Acts 6:3 and the concern with biblical goals in Acts 15:17. In each case, not merely order but the good of all those involved is apparent.

Leadership Toward Biblical Goals

Too often those who are concerned with the care of God's flock become so involved with immediate needs such as the visitation of the sick, planning and conducting meetings, and dealing with spiritual problems, that they fail to exercise fully their responsibility of leadership. Elders' meetings, like prayer meetings, tend to be taken up with matters needing immediate attention and, to use a medical metaphor, the church is constantly coping with epidemics rather than engaging in preventative medicine.

Leadership is concerned not merely with the maintenance of an orderly *status quo*, but with the fulfilment of biblical goals, those purposes which God has for the church. We are not left with uncertainty as to what these are, for they are expressed clearly in Scripture, especially in the Ephesian letter. The opening chapter of this epistle is overflowing with various expressions which convey both the fact and the content of God's purpose: 'chosen . . . that we should be . . . He destined us . . . according to the purpose of His will . . . He has made known to us . . . the mystery of His will, according to His purpose . . . as a plan for the fulness of time, to unite all things in Him . . . according to the purpose of Him who accomplishes all things according to the counsel of His will.' The rest of this chapter, and the whole epistle, reflects this sense of ultimate purpose and meaning for the church, which exists for 'the praise of His glory' (1:12). Even now the 'manifold wisdom of God' is being displayed 'according to the eternal purpose which He has realized in Christ Jesus our Lord' (3:10f).

To such magnificent realities the church's leadership should respond with the call, 'Rise up, O men of God, be done with lesser things!' The fourth chapter does just this in the challenge to 'lead a life worthy of the calling to which you have been called'. There follows another series of goals, this time directly related to the daily life of the church. We are to become mature in knowledge and mature in our mutual relationships. That is, we seek the 'unity of the faith', as each part of the body of Christ 'builds itself up in love'.

It has been said that evangelists (Eph 4:11) contribute to church growth by augmentation, while pastors and teachers produce growth through edification. But this edification is not accomplished overnight. There are a number of intermediate goals to which the church leaders should devote themselves, which in turn will effect the long range goals and ultimately the divine purposes for the church. The passages we have already considered relating to the work of elders indicate that teaching and admonishing are the elders' concern. This also implies correction of error (Titus 1:9, 13). The pastoral function of elders includes a concern for the physical, mental and spiritual health of everyone who is in the fellowship of, and under the discipline of, the local church. That is, everything which affects a believer's relationship to other believers and to his Lord, everything which affects his progress toward those goals which constitute the will of God for the church is the concern of elders.

One intermediate goal is the proper functioning of the body of Christ. This involves helping each person to recognize his own gifts, 'natural' (given through heredity and environment) and 'spiritual' (given directly by the Spirit). Wise elders will build on the strengths of individuals, not dwelling on their weaknesses, helping each one to find a spiritual service for which he is fitted by God. Wherever possible, they will delegate responsibility (and the appropriate authority) to faithful younger believers. They will see to it that the whole work of the church is done without undue overlapping or omission, just as they make sure that the whole counsel of God is taught. Areas of responsibility will be clearly defined. Communication will be maintained so that each knows what the other is seeking to accomplish and how the work of each contributes to the overall purpose of the church.

In this way a sense of fellowship and unity will be encouraged. Elders will follow the example of the Lord Jesus, who called his disciples 'friends' because he shared the meaning of his work with them (John 15:15), and of Paul who referred to his co-workers in terms indicating association rather than subordination. They will listen as well as speak, building the will to work and encouraging the use of gifts for the common good and the Lord's glory (Rom. 12:I Cor. 12).

This involves a sense of discipleship, which in turn implies making others disciples (Matt. 28:19). It means a concern for individuals, spending time especially with 'faithful men' who will in turn teach others (II Tim. 2:2). Leaders, as well as disciples, must be trained. Opportunities for various ministries must be provided. All too often promising individuals are kept in routine jobs which do not stimulate growth. While it is true that he who would lead must first learn to serve, and granted that to some degree 'a man's gift will make place for him', it is the elders' responsibilitity to observe those who are faithful and provide further spiritual opportunities.

Leadership of the church is not a 'spare time' job, even if it must be part time, beyond those hours devoted to daily work and family responsibilities. By example and teaching, elders must express the deep conviction that we are to 'seek first the kingdom of God'. Priorities must be set and constantly reviewed. What worked in the past may not meet the needs of present and future. Principles and methods must constantly be extricated from each other, with the former reaffirmed and taught, and the latter re-evaluated. The time must be redeemed and specific attainable goals kept before the church.

Leadership is thus concerned with the future, that is to say, with the accomplishment of God's will 'to the praise of the glory of His grace'. Leadership and authority in the church exist essentially that we might bring to him 'glory in the church and in Christ Jesus to all generations, for ever and ever' (Eph. 3:21).

NOTES

1 F. F. Bruce, *A New Testament Commentary* (1969), p. 637

2 *The New International Dictionary of New Testament Theology* ed. Colin Brown 1 (1975), pp. 188–192 (with extensive bibliography)

4

Worship

ALAN G. NUTE

Definition

Worship is an encounter between God and man: God reveals Himself and man responds. In its widest sense, this response embraces virtually all those activities of the church which are dealt with in this volume. At its narrowest, worship is restricted to 'adoration'. The meaning given to it in this contribution will lie somewhere between these two extremes.

The etymologies of the Hebrew and Greek words employed for worship reveal two strands: to serve, and to bow down or to prostrate oneself. As for the English word, this is derived from the Anglo-Saxon *weorthscipe*, which, in due course, became 'worthship', signifying to ascribe worth or value to something or someone. Linguistically, it is invalid to derive the current meaning of a word from its etymological history. In this case, however, etymological history and current meaning happen to coincide. Thus the worship of God may be seen to be an appreciation by the worshipper of His infinite worth, an appreciation which is expressed by bowing low in adoration and then by going forth in His service. It reveals a relationship between the worshipper and the One worshipped. Worship becomes an encounter.

Worship and Revelation

In the church's worship this encounter consists of revelation on God's part and of a corresponding response on the part of the congregation. Our immediate concern is with the latter. Even so, it is essential to bear in mind that response can never be divorced from revelation. The latter is indispensable to the former, and they must be held in equipoise.

40

It is wrong to place such emphasis on revelation as imparted through the preaching of the Word that little or no opportunity is afforded the congregation for making their response in corporate praise to God. On the other hand, to provide no place for revelation through the Scriptures when God's people are gathered to worship Him is equally mistaken. Strange as it may seem, this has been asserted by some to be unnecessary and even improper. Such an attitude probably stems from the notion that the needed revelation is already the possession of the Christian congregation; or that each worshipper may properly be expected to have made prior, personal, spiritual preparation. Where these questionable assumptions are made, worship becomes limited almost entirely to response, and that in the nature of adoration.

A prime reason for stressing the importance of the Scriptures in public worship is to fulfil the stipulation Jesus makes: 'Those who worship', He says, 'must worship . . . in truth' (John 4:24). The significance of this in relation to the sincerity of the worshipper will be considered later. Meanwhile, it should be noted that the context indicates that the saying applies equally to that necessary accuracy of belief which determines our worship. Worship can so easily be governed by tradition. It was so for the woman of Samaria. She conceded that for her it was dictated by the beliefs and practices of her 'fathers' (v. 20). Jesus insisted that true worship must be based on revelation. 'We worship what we know, for salvation is of the Jews' (v. 22). God's saving work in and for His people proved to be both the ground and the spring of worship. This principle is an abiding one. 'True worshippers will worship ... in ... truth' (v. 23). Westcott aptly comments on this statement, 'Worship is necessarily limited by the idea of the being worshipped. A true idea of God is essential.'[1] We have the 'true idea of God' given us in Scripture.

If we are to worship 'in truth', it is to be expected that the Word will be given a place of prominence in public worship. It is the great safeguard against all that is false. Vain worship, Jesus taught, is the result of replacing 'the commandment of God' with 'the tradition of men' (Mark 7:7, 8). The revelation of God in the Bible is that which will preserve our worship from becoming superficial, inadequate and therefore unworthy. Moreover, the scriptural presentation of His glory, of His utter holiness and of the greatness of His grace will produce the twin virtues of awe and humility without which true worship is not possible.

To neglect the Bible in worship is also derogatory to God. By omitting the element of revelation we belittle God's part in worship and extol man's. Thus we ignore the fact that the initiative is always with Him. We also fail to appreciate aright that His desire is to awaken our love for Him by a fresh disclosure of His love for us. The objection that is sometimes made, that we come not to get but to give, is a dangerous half-truth. Worship is always reciprocal.

Another consequence of not giving to Scripture its proper place is to limit response, in large measure, to a past appreciation of the Lord and His grace. This tends to spiritual staleness. There is nothing to rival the Word for the way in which it stimulates the soul to praise. In a booklet entitled *Soul Nourishment First*, George Muller tells how commencing his devotions with a meditation in Holy Scripture produced a revolutionary effect upon his times of personal communion with God. He found this practice the cure for spiritual barrenness and lack of concentration, as well as the means whereby 'my heart being nourished by the truth, being brought into experimental fellowship with God, I speak to my Father and to my Friend (vile though I am and unworthy of it) about the things that He has brought before me in His precious Word'. A judicious use of Scripture could have a similar effect upon the church at worship, moving the company to a vital, spontaneous expression of praise.

One further important reason for setting before the gathered church some aspect of the truth of God as revealed in the Word is that the worship to which we are called is a corporate activity. In his *Principles of Christian Worship*, Raymond Abba speaks of 'a legacy of nineteenth-century atomistic individualism which destroys the essentially corporate nature of Christian worship.' He adds, 'Worship is a united act; it is not the sum-total of a number of concurrent individual acts of devotion.'[2] Clearly, there needs to be a co-ordinating factor. This is to be found in Scripture and in particular as the Spirit through it fulfils the ministry which Jesus attributed to Him. 'He will glorify Me, He will take what is Mine and declare it to you' (John 16:14). This effects a concentration of thought and produces a sense of direction, so that the various contributions in praise and thanksgiving become coherent and purposeful. In this way the service becomes more meaningful for the worshippers and more worthy of Him whose glory is thus set forth.

It should be added that every facet of Divine self-revelation is appropriate as a subject for the church's contemplation in its desire to offer acceptable worship. God is to be praised both for His wonderful works of creation and for His mighty deeds in history; but, most especially, for what He has done in Jesus Christ, and what He will do ultimately through Him.[3] Psalmist and prophet express their adoration of Him as both the God of creation and the Lord of history. They recount exultantly His manifold works in the earth around and in the heavens above (Ps. 104; Isa. 40:12–14). They sing His praise whose providential dealings with His covenant people and with the nations proclaim His sovereign power (Ps. 105, Isa. 40:15–17, 21–24). In heaven, too, God is worshipped as creator (Rev. 4:6–8) and Lord of history (Rev. 5:1–10). These particular features of Divine self-revelation could well receive a greater attention than is normally the case in the present worship of the church.

In heaven's worship the Redeemer-Lamb is central. So must He be in the congregation of the saints on earth. It is in Him that revelation comes to its completion and in His reconciling work that it finds its apex. To behold Him is to worship. Thus Isaiah 'saw His glory' and worshipped (John 12:41; Isa. 6:1–8). John, too, confronted with the exalted Christ 'fell at His feet as though dead' (Rev. 1:17). and if it is asked where we may view Him, the answer is supplied by the hymnwriter—'And in Thy Book revealed, I see *Thee* Lord'.

43

In the light of the foregoing considerations, there is surely a strong case for a reading and a brief meditation in Holy Scripture as a prelude to the time of worship. Such evidence as there is in the record both of the institution and of the subsequent observance of the Lord's Supper would support this practice (John 13–15; Acts 20:7). This is not to advocate or defend the view that a formal teaching ministry should always be associated with 'the breaking of bread'. While many arguments could be adduced in its support, it is a separate issue and lies outside the scope of this chapter. Our concern here is with the importance of the Bible in public worship as that which regulates, inspires and co-ordinates the praise God's people offer.

'Form' and 'Breath' in Worship

We must now turn from the question of revelation in worship to consider more closely the nature of our response. This, too, is the work of God. As such it bears two features which can be traced back to the very beginning of God's life-imparting activities. The creation of man is described in Genesis 2:7 as follows: 'Then the Lord God formed man of dust from the ground, and breathed into his nostrils the breath of life; and man became a living being.' It may be said that wherever there is true life these two features of 'form' and 'breath' are necessarily present. This certainly applies to worship.

Under the old covenant, the form of worship divinely prescribed was one of great complexity and richness. It consisted of specified places and times, of consecrated personnel and above all of a detailed and deeply significant ritual. To be acceptable, worship had, on the one hand, to conform to the requirements laid down; and on the other, it had to be marked by sincerity on the part of the worshipper. The tragedy that dogged Israel's worship was that they concentrated on 'form' and ignored 'breath'. Priests and people alike were punctilious as far as the externals were concerned, but seriously neglected that which was inward and spiritual. This charge is constantly levelled against them by the prophets (I Sam. 15:22; Ps. 40:6–8; 51:16, 17; Isa. 1:12–17; Jer. 7:21–23; Mic. 6:6–8).

With the coming of Christ the Old Testament ritual of worship was fulfilled and has, therefore, been abolished. A new day has dawned in which 'place' is of no significance, as Jesus makes plain (John 4:21). Nor is 'time' (Rom. 14:5). Now, all are priests who are Christ's (I Pet. 2:5). The New Testament will be searched in vain for anything remotely like a ceremonial procedure for the church at worship. And yet, sadly, the conflict between 'form' and 'breath' remains. 'It is perhaps worthwhile to remark', writes C. F. D. Moule, 'that the whole history of worship might be written round the fascinating and difficult question of the relation between the outward and the inward.'[4] Doubtless the greatest danger still rests in too great an emphasis on the outward. How salutary is Charles Hodge's comment on Romans 2:25, 'Whenever true religion declines, the disposition to lay undue stress on external rites is increased.'[5]

While alert to this danger the church must at the same time recognize that a living response of worship requires 'form' as well as 'breath'. Place, time and order are not of the essence of worship; but congregational worship is impossible without them. A correct evaluation will be preserved by an appreciation of the attention given these things in the New Testament. The meeting-place for the church at worship was determined by local circumstances. That they met in a known venue is obvious. As for the time when they gathered, apart from the fact that this was on the first day of the week (John 20:19, 20; Acts 20:7; I Cor. 16:2) little is known of the hour.

What of the order of service? Here again no 'pattern' can be established either from the Acts' record or from the Epistles. The picture that emerges is of a composite service in which prayers and praises were offered, hymns sung, the Scripture read and expounded, the Lord's supper observed and a collection taken. It has been suggested that Acts 2.42 'represents the course of early Christian worship'[6] with 'the apostles' teaching' followed by a fellowship-meal and 'the breaking of bread', concluding with the 'the prayers'. In all probability this one service on the Lord's day would be the sole opportunity for Christians to assemble.

In our different, and perhaps more favoured circumstances, we tend to allocate the various church activities to separate occasions. It is essential to keep in mind that this arrangement is purely one of current, practical expediency and for this reason must be kept flexible. No importance should be attached to the separation of these spiritual exercises nor one exercise elevated over against another.

At the heart of the church's worship will be the celebration of the Lord's Supper. Nothing sets forth so eloquently or brings to mind more vividly the Saviour's passion. It is an acted parable, the meaning of which Jesus Himself provided in His words of institution. In obedience to His command, thus to remember Him, the feast is kept. Remembrance, however, does not exhaust its significance. A careful survey of those Scriptures which describe the institution, the practice and the spiritual implications of 'the breaking of bread' will reveal that it bears a much fuller import than is commonly attached to it. It has been asserted that 'the New Testament Eucharist differed from and had fuller significance than its modern counterpart'.[7] Where this is so, it should be remedied!

In the worship which accompanies the observance of the Lord's Supper the following facts should be kept constantly in mind. It assures us that Christ's death, being for the remission of sins, brings us into covenant relationship with God (Matt. 26:28). It makes moral demands upon us (I Cor. 10:21). It requires us to recognize the one body of Christ and to discharge our responsibilities as members of it (I Cor. 10:16, 17, 31–33). It challenges us to renewed commitment to Christ as Lord (I Cor. 10:22). It focuses thought upon the return in glory of our great God and Saviour Jesus Christ and sets forth with uncommon potency the message of the gospel (I Cor. 11:26).

Nothing further requires to be said about the form of worship, except to add that each service must have 'form', even if only to comply with the requirement that 'all things should be done decently and in order' (I Cor. 14:40). The nature of the order will be dictated solely by the determination to provide an arrangement which best serves the end of giving to the Lord the glory due to His name. However flexible it may be, order is essential if there is to be corporate worship. Without it, there is confusion. And 'God is not a God of confusion but of peace' (v. 33).

The Spirit in Worship

A 'form' without 'breath' is a corpse. In the same way, a church is lifeless which boasts a form of worship corresponding to an imagined New Testament prototype, yet lacks the breath of the Spirit. In His memorable instruction on the subject, Jesus is emphatic concerning the indispensability of the Spirit in worship. 'God is spirit,' He says, 'and those who worship Him must worship in spirit and truth.' There are two insights here. First, worship is the product of the interaction of the Divine Spirit and the human spirit. Second, true worship will be marked by complete sincerity.

Of the first, Paul writes in Philippians 3:3. The text ('worship God in spirit') and the marginal reading ('worship by the Spirit of God') describe complementary activities. Thus the Holy Spirit operates upon the highest region of man's being to beget that response to God which is pure worship.

Gathered to worship, the church will plead the promise of her Lord: 'When the Spirit of truth comes, He will guide you into all the truth . . . He will glorify Me, for He will take what is Mine and declare it to you' (John 16:13, 14). Where this is experienced the worshippers enjoy an ever fresh appreciation of Christ. Moreover, their expressions of praise are characterized by spontaneity, for 'where the Spirit of the Lord is, there is freedom' (II Cor. 3:17).

Paul felt it incumbent upon him, however, to emphasize that the spirit we have received is 'a spirit of . . . self-control' (II Tim. 1:7). In the church at Corinth liberty was rapidly degenerating into licence. Freedom for the Spirit to move sovereignly in the congregation at worship was in danger of being distorted into freedom for each individual to act as he wished, the pretext being that the worshipper was under the compulsion of the Spirit. Hence the apostolic statement that 'the spirits of prophets are subject to prophets' (I Cor. 14:32).

Much misunderstanding surrounds what is commonly called 'the leading of the Spirit'. Despite the fact that the phrase is not so used in the New Testament, it is frequently applied in a special way to services for worship. Christians certainly need to be directed by the Spirit when engaging in congregational praise to God, but not, let it be said, in any fashion peculiar to that occasion. There is no biblical warrant for the notion that believers need to be led by the Spirit in some other way, or to some greater degree, than when engaged in the ordinary business of daily living. Romans 8:14 teaches that such leading is the hallmark of sonship and Galatians 5:18 that it evidences a life freed from the harsh dominion of the law.

As to the way in which the Holy Spirit directs, it has been well said that 'His leading is intimately linked with, and operates in association with, the exercise of spiritual judgment on the believer's part'.[8] Paul himself deplored the divorcing of spirit and intellect when engaged in public thanksgiving to God (I Cor. 14:15). Writing on this subject John Stott comments, 'In all true worship the mind must be fully and fruitfully engaged.'[9]

In addition, to assert that a service of 'open worship' is under the leading of the Spirit in a way in which a prearranged one is not has no basis in Scripture. This is true whether the prearrangement has been agreed or is tacit. In imparting direction, the Spirit is not limited by the time factor. Jesus assured His disciples that in certain emergency situations they could count on the instant help of the Spirit (Matt. 10:19, 20). Meetings of believers for worship hardly come into this category. There is no special sanctity in immediacy. The Spirit-led individual will be ready to offer on one occasion what has been recalled to mind at the particular moment, and on another what has been premeditated. One way or another, it is the duty of all, by the Spirit's aid, to come to worship with heart and mind prepared.

If the non-structured service in no way guarantees the presence and activity of the Holy Spirit, it certainly requires it. Moreover, the organizing of the worship from start to finish will prove no solution for the gathering that lacks the evident power of the Spirit. There must be both 'form' and 'breath'—or to borrow Oscar Cullmann's words, a 'harmonious combination of freedom and restriction' in which 'there lies the greatness and uniqueness of the early Christian service of worship'.[10]

Spiritual Sacrifices

The spiritual nature of worship finds emphasis in I Peter 2:4–10. We are reminded that all who have 'come to Him' are constituted 'a holy priesthood'. Each is qualified 'to offer spiritual sacrifices', and we are not left in the dark as to the sacrifices which, in this age, are acceptable to God. The church will 'offer-up a sacrifice of praise' (Heb. 13:15). This will be in 'psalms and hymns and spiritual songs' (Col. 3:16) and also as one and another lead the congregation in worship. Nothing will aid the individual in the discharge of this responsibility like a mind stored with the truth of God and a heart moved by the grace of God. The tendency to preach in prayer must be strenuously resisted. At the same time it is plain that they worship most acceptably who find in Scripture the content of their praise, and often the words as well.

There are additional sacrifices to be offered and these may well prove the sincerity of our verbal worship. They include the sharing of our possessions, whether in cash or in kind, with the needy (I Cor. 16:2; Phil. 4:14–18; Heb. 13:16), the work of evangelism (Rom. 15:16), a total commitment to a life of holiness and of obedience to the will of God (Rom. 12:1, 2) and, for some, even martyrdom itself (Phil. 2:17; II Tim. 4:6). The exhortation 'Little children, let us not love in word or speech but in deed and in truth' (I John 3:18) applies in a special way to worship.

The sincerity which is required if we are to worship 'in spirit and in truth' consists also in holiness of character. A Holy God insists that it be 'a holy priesthood' that offers 'spiritual sacrifices' (I Pet. 2:5). This stipulation finds constant emphasis from Genesis to Revelation; thus the intending worshipper meets continually verses such as Lev. 10:3; Ps. 24:3–6; 26:6; Matt. 5:23, 24; I Cor. 5:6–8; and Heb. 10:22; as well as the searching words contained in those passages in I Corinthians concerning the Lord's Supper (10:14–22; 11:27–32). On John 4:24, Alford comments, 'With no by-ends nor hypocritical regards, but in truth and earnestness.'[11] 'The Lord is near to all who call upon Him . . . in truth' (Ps. 145:18).

Finally no statement in the discourse of John chapter 4 is more arresting and affecting than this: 'For such the Father *seeks* to worship Him' (v. 23). Jesus had earlier assured the woman that the water He could supply would satisfy completely. From this spring she may drink and never thirst again. Later, when talking to His disciples He referred to the fact that for Him 'to do the will of Him who sent Me, and to accomplish His work' was as 'food to eat' (vv. 32, 34). He found it an infinitely satisfying experience. And, yet, neither of these references to desire and satisfaction is as striking as this suggestion, that by offering worship in spirit and in truth we may answer a deep longing in the heart of God. The Father *seeks* worshippers. Overwhelming as the thought is, the Old Testament anticipates it. Moses is bidden to 'Command the people of Israel, and say to them, "My offering, my *food* for my offerings by fire, my pleasing odour, you shall take heed to offer me in its due season"' (Num. 28:2); and sacrifices are called 'the bread of your God' (Lev. 21:8).

The invitation, then, is that we respond to the Father's desire and worship Him in spirit and in truth. There is no loftier privilege, no nobler exercise, than this.

NOTES

1 B. F. Westcott, *Gospel of St. John* (1882). *in loc.*
2 R. Abba, *Principles of Christian Worship* (1957), p. 86

3 C. F. D. Moule, *Worship in the New Testament* (1969), p. 31

4 Moule, *Worship*, p. 31

5 Charles Hodge, *Commentary on the Epistle to the Romans* (1886), p. 68

6 J. Jeremias, quoted by Moule, *Worship*, p. 18

7 John A. Simpson, 'The Local Church—A Worshipping Community' [Synopsis], Christian Brethren Research Fellowship (n.d.)

8 Raymond Aitchison, 'The Leading of the Spirit and the Lord's Supper' *The Witness* 92 (1962), p. 403

9 J. R. W. Stott, *Your Mind Matters* (1972), p. 27

10 Oscar Culmann, *Early Christian Worship* (1953), p. 33

11 Henry Alford, *The New Testament for English Readers* (1856), *in loc.*

5

Pastoral Care and Church Discipline

ROBERT LIGHTBODY

The Calling of the Shepherd

Ever since the sons of Jacob said to Pharaoh, 'Your servants are shepherds' (Gen. 47:3), both that calling and those engaged in it have gained fair mention, in the Bible at least, by those who recall old times. The historic theme reached its peak in David; in him the Shepherd was enthroned. Thereafter, things fell away badly and shepherds were not the same. People, instead of looking back, began to look forward. Ezekiel, when captive in Babylon, was one of these forward-looking men. For his part, he was certain that, despite appearances, God Himself would come to the rescue of His people and would in due time raise up a shepherd who would tend his flock as no previous notable shepherd had ever done (Ezek. 34:16, 22, 23). When, as it turned out, that Shepherd arrived, He was vexed by what He saw. It was as though His flock had never had shepherds at all; harassed and helpless, it was indiscriminately scattered upon the mountains of Israel (Matt. 9:36). This flock of His was of a special kind, made up as it was of men and women, lost souls. John 10 gives us the self-portrait of the Heavenly Shepherd. Sad to say, the people to whom He came did not recognise Him, just as today the world for which He died cares little about Him. John the Baptist addresses our world as well as his own when he protests, 'Among you stands one whom you do not know' (John 1:26). To those who have heard His voice and know it, things are altogether different: His seeking, His finding, His loving and His dying are indelibly engraved on the fleshy tables of their hearts. In

Peter's words, they know the blessedness of having returned to 'the Shepherd and Guardian of their souls' (I Pet. 2:25).

In Pharaoh's sophisticated world shepherds had no status. Shepherds were an economic write-off, their work did not increase the Gross National Product and so their calling was brushed aside as being of little real moment. In our age, even among believers, the occupation of a shepherd (spiritually considered) is regarded by many as of questionable value. And so what is of paramount importance in the eyes of Heaven is lightly regarded on earth. The Great Shepherd appoints under-shepherds, and gives them charge of His sheep (I Pet. 5:2–4). His gifts are that 'some' should be pastors and teachers (Eph. 4:11). If the word 'some' in this verse is understood as introducing each class of gifted persons, then it will be seen that 'pastor and teacher' is a double gift in one and the same individual.

Pastors are spiritual shepherds and their sheep are those who have been born again. Their duty is not only to care for the sheep, but also to correct them. Thus the subject of pastoral care is closely linked with that of discipline, for these are but equally important aspects of the same job.

The Attitude Necessary for Spiritual Shepherding

God's people are the 'apple of His eye' and have to be taken care of with unremitting industry. Like the Good Shepherd who said, 'I know my own', the under-shepherd must also know his sheep. To quote Edwin Hatch, 'To each shepherd a portion of the Lord's flock has been assigned, and his account must be rendered to his own master.' We, not infrequently, castigate Jacob; but, with all his faults, he was an outstanding shepherd. Anger makes his prose poetic as he thus expostulates with Laban: 'These twenty years I have been with you; . . . I bore the loss of it myself . . . thus I was; by day the heat consumed me, and the cold by night' (Gen. 31:38–40 RSV). There is but one Shepherd who never loses any sheep (John 17:12). Some who are called shepherds are 'hirelings' and do not have what it takes to be true shepherds. For spiritual shepherding is a tiring, costly, time-consuming

53

business, as well as a full-time occupation. To get to know people, to discover what really lies behind a face, and, as a friend and confidant, to get men and women to share their hidden problems and troubles is a difficult and long-term task.

Only a minority of the people of God have ever been suited for the job. Real shepherds were scarce in ancient Israel, and they are scarce today. This is a baffling problem of both past and present. It is illustrated by Timothy, during whose lifetime there must have been quite a number in the churches who professed to be shepherds; but Paul had no option but to send him to Philippi with the sad admission that 'there is no one else here, who sees things as I do, and takes a genuine interest in your concerns; they are all bent on their own ends, not on the cause of Jesus Christ' (Phil. 2:20 NEB). Philippians 2 is about the poured-out life; it speaks of self-emptying. It shows the Lord Jesus, Paul himself, Timothy and Epaphroditus neglecting self-interest for the sake of others—

> Others, Lord, yes, others,
> Let this my motto be.
> Help me to live for others,
> That I may live like Thee.

Therefore, only by breathing out such sentiments sincerely and under the constraining power and grace of the Holy Spirit and being deeply conscious of the implications should anyone 'desire the office of a bishop' (I Tim. 3:1).

The Ministry of the Under-Shepherd in the Church
Through a variety of circumstances, many of the Lord's people are deprived either temporarily or permanently of Church fellowship. The shepherds must visit them, and more wisdom and tact is required for this than many possess. It is singularly unhelpful to bombard the afflicted, the downcast or the physically weak with random texts from the Bible. At the same time, 'A word fitly spoken is like apples of gold in a

setting of silver' (Prov. 25:11). Faced with the calamities of life it is sometimes best to say very little, if anything at all.

A few years ago I heard a powerful address by one whose home had seen a good deal of physical suffering. The point made was that 'Job's comforters' were so named because, though they had really no solution to offer, they insisted in trying to find one. Life, even for the Christian, presents problems concerning which no man has an answer; therefore, it is well to keep in mind that in the crucible of trial words often make things worse. When he is called upon to minister to the needs of one who, for all his faith, has had just about as much as he can possibly take, the wise pastor can take comfort that there is in Heaven one who can be 'touched with the feeling of our infirmities' (Heb. 4:15). Faber puts it very aptly when he wrote:

> There is no place where earth's sorrows
> Are more felt than up in Heaven.
> There is no place where earth's failings
> Have such kindly judgment given.

Under-shepherds must always be examples to the flock. Paul told Timothy, 'Set the believers an example in speech and conduct, in love, in faith, in purity' (I Tim. 4:12). By any standards this is a tall order. When, however, others begin to look upon pastors as models of God-glorifying conduct, they can be content that God's grace has not been entirely lost upon them. This, in itself, proves that the gospel can change people radically.

Further, the pastor-teacher has to feed the sheep, and the food is the Word of God. Not just some of Scripture, but all of it. A restricted diet will not do, for constant feeding does not always equal true nourishment. Just as all good dieticians study the physical needs of all those for whom they are responsible, so those who prepare spiritual food must apportion the food wisely. They must weigh, measure, calculate and mix that which is suitable to the needs of those under their care. All necessary ingredients must be included in the diet lest the sheep should be permanently stunted in growth.

The whole counsel of God must be declared to all the people of God (Acts 20:27; I Tim. 3:14–17). When different age-groups are included and opposite sexes are involved this is not easy. Timothy was enjoined by Paul to conduct himself in a manner appropriate to his relationship with the people with whom he was dealing, and by extension this principle applies to pastors of every age. One's plain duty is to 'proclaim the message and press it home on all occasions, convenient or inconvenient' (II Tim. 4:2 NEB). One should omit nothing contained in the teaching of God's Word, should be courteous and patient with all.

Study I Thessalonians and you will see Paul himself as an example. Under the acknowledged scrutiny of God and men, he declares that he dealt with new converts one by one, first as a mother and then as a father, for they were his very own children. One who has led a person to Christ will never treat him harshly. Paul not only preached the gospel, he poured out his soul. He laboured night and day. The merest whimper of the smallest babe in Christ had but to reach him through the pagan air, and he was up attending to its need, thus proving to every lisping convert that 'grace is free' (I Thess. 2:12). Thus young Christians learned 'the meekness and gentleness of Christ' from Paul. Caring means sharing. The work of pastors as set out in this epistle is to 'admonish the idle, encourage the fainthearted, help the weak and be patient with all' (I Thess. 5:1–12).

Worthy of Double Honour

Arduous labours are the lot of those who undertake pastoral responsibility. It is little wonder therefore that those who benefit from this toil are told to honour their benefactors, and to do it in a two-fold manner. They must be held in high esteem and be loved for their work's sake. That is the first step. But these God-given men may be further honoured in another way and that is to provide them 'with the means necessary for their support' (I Tim. 5:17). Hort makes the point in his *Christian Ecclesia* that as we read how the early Church proceeded what we have to guide us is a history and not a law. As things developed for them they adapted, under God, scriptural principles to each new situation; and so must we. Many assemblies are languishing today because many elders are trying to do on a part-time basis what is in fact a full-time job. The result is that pastoral work is simply neglected. Paul was often hampered in his ministry by niggardliness. Did he not work with his own hands and put his hand into his own pocket to support fellow workers from the proceeds? For like his Master before him, he would not demand from the Lord's people what was not freely and willingly given. Imagine having to answer to God for putting the brakes on Paul! But even today men who are much needed in pastoral ministry in many local churches are forced to engage in secular work for their own support, to the manifest detriment of the Lord's people.

Among assemblies of Brethren, 'pastor' is often an emotive word, when it should not be. In its context, it is just as scriptural a term as 'evangelist', and no amount of side-stepping will take away from its divine sanction. In very many cases, it seems some would prefer that pastoral duties were not carried out at all than that we should make it financially possible for gifted and experienced men to give their whole time to it! Paul at Corinth, Timothy at Ephesus and Titus in Crete furnish clear and unmistakable New Testament precedent for a settled pastoral ministry, at least for a protracted period of time. The low moral tone in the churches in Crete called for urgent action from Titus, and there are many parallels in the modern situation for those who have eyes to see them. In the Church at Philippi, there were bishops, deacons and serving missionaries, together with the whole congregation (Phil. 1:1). Given all that, why did Paul send Timothy back there to do pastoral work? Concerning I Timothy 3:1, Lilley writes, ' "Episcopate" or "office of a bishop" though etymologically accurate, is really inadmissible, because it suggests the features of "singularity in succession and superiority in ordination", which had no place in the primitive conception of the office. "Pastorate" comes much nearer the mark; but it also points to an individualisation of the function in the single teaching elder, which though clearly countenanced, had not as yet been fully realised. The official here spoken of was one of a body, that was jointly responsible for "the oversight of the flock".' On this theme Hort adds, ' "Elder" is the title, "oversight" is the function to be exercised by the holder of the title within the Ecclesia.'

The Necessity for Church Discipline

Now let us turn to the second aspect of the work for which the under-shepherd must also assume responsibility, the remedial measures which from time to time become necessary. Only self-disciplined men have the moral right to correct others, for, in this as in all else, only the taught can teach. A. G. Clarke, writes aptly, 'In Eastern lands a shepherd is not a driver, but a leader of the sheep.' The world may reject former and well-proved codes for living, but the people of God must remember that 'whatsoever things were written aforetime were written for our learning' (Rom. 15:4). God's standards are not subject to change, neither is their validity or relevance impaired by the fluctuating opinions of men who refuse to have their appetites curbed. It is necessary to keep in mind the implied imperatives of John's First Epistle, as he sums up for us the will of God for His children: *Believe! Behave! Be Loving!*

Those who have to bring discipline to bear on others must do so with a certain mental predisposition and exhibit what Ellicott styles 'the well-balanced state of mind arising from habitual self-restraint'. Scripture enjoins upon pastors that they act 'soberly', 'temperately' and 'discretely'. 'A man must', comments Lilley, 'live prudently towards himself, righteously towards others, and piously towards God, remembering also that the time of this present age has been shortened' (I Cor. 7:33). The world, with all its attraction, is on the way out, God will deal with its wanton ways. In the meantime, God disciplines us his children that we may not be condemned with the world (I John 2:17; I Cor. 11:32). The teaching elder should, therefore, be guided by constant recourse to the Word of God and seek to be of pure motive as he applies divinely appointed sanctions to the conduct of his own life and the lives of the people of God who are under his care.

Very often discipline and righteousness are associated in the Bible, and this is no accident. The grace of God that brings salvation teaches us that 'denying ungodliness and worldly lusts, we should live soberly, righteously, and godly, in this present world' (Titus 2:12). At the present time, for many reasons we seem, as individuals and congregations, to neglect the Scriptures 'which are profitable for discipline, which is in righteousness' (II Tim. 3:16). The twelfth chapter of the Epistle to the Hebrews is without doubt the classic passage on personal discipline. It is because God loves us, because we are His children, that He corrects us. The process is not pleasant; but ultimately, if we learn by it, it yields the peaceable fruit of righteousness. The tone of the life of any church is set by the quality of life of each of its members. God's discipline is toward the goal of our sharing in His holiness (Heb. 12:5, 6, 11).

Different Categories of Offenders

How are we to deal with those church members whose way of life runs counter to the Christian way? Different forms of correction apply to distinct categories of offenders.

First, there is the problem of the person who has done something wrong on a sudden impulse (Gal. 6:1–3 NEB). Satan sees to it that we are surrounded by traps suitably baited. The person here in view has been snared and injured, and so as a member of the body of Christ he cannot effectively function; in this passage he is likened to an incapacitated limb. John Stott is very helpful on this chapter. He asks a series of questions: 'What to do?' 'Who is to do it?' 'How should it be done?' 'What if it were done?' In answer to the first question, he quotes the Lord and Paul. 'Gain him,' said the Saviour. 'Restore him', advises Paul. Since the answers to the first three questions are found in the first verse, it should be memorised. The answer to the second question is this: the 'spiritual' are to nurse the brother back to health. J. H. Large likens the local Church to a hospital in which there must be 'a special ward of grace, where souls can receive personal treatment as inpatients'. Galatians 6 is that ward. The attendants, though men of like passions with the patient and conscious of their own weakness and proneness to sin, are gentle in their treatment of the injured one. It has been rightly noticed that 'only the spiritual are gentle'. This answers question number three. Finally, if maimed brethren were so treated, what would the outcome be? Here is how one commentator sees it: 'Unkind gossip would be avoided; more serious backsliding prevented; the good of the church advanced; and the Name of Christ glorified.'

Secondly come those whose misdemeanours merely call for censure. Wherein have these erred? Hogg and Vine suggest that they may be guilty of 'idleness, officiousness or excitability'. Paul reprimands the Corinthians for an offence which is of the same order; they were 'biting the hand that fed them', and it was a divinely ordained hand (I Cor. 4:14; I Thess. 5:12, 14; Rom. 15:14). Should, however, they pay no heed to a verbal warning, further action has to be taken against them. Paul suggests that we should avoid association with such people (II Thess. 3:14). If due deference is not paid to this biblical pattern, factions will result and divisions will occur (Rom. 16:17, 18).

Scripture also indicates that the activities of certain would-be teachers must be curbed. Too often today such people are treated as unavoidable, or worse still as a joke; and while the elders hesitate, our young people with more perception find fellowship elsewhere, realising that such conduct is inappropriate to the house of God. Those who teach that which should not be taught and others who stand up to speak when they possess no gift for preaching must be disciplined (Titus 1:9–14; I Cor. 14:26–29). The first type act contrary to sound doctrine, and the second group, by self-obtrusion, 'Quench the Spirit' in others (I Thess. 5:19; Hogg and Vine) and thus prevent things being done decently and in order.

Those so far considered have been subject to correction

inside the local Church and away from the eyes of the world. As a last resort, persistent evil-doers have to be excommunicated. The procedure would seem to be that the elders must first impartially investigate the case. Then, the congregation, being informed of the charge and the judgment, should agree with both. E. Tipson believes that a special meeting of the Church should be convened to carry out the act of excommunication. Two classes of people are liable to this fate: those consistently guilty of gross moral evil and false teachers. In the first category are not only those who are guilty of extra or premarital sexual relations (as I Cor. 5:10–13 clearly shows), but other sins must be taken into account. And as A. G. Clarke has said, 'Evil doctrine can be more harmful than loose living, if for no other reason than that the latter is usually recognized sooner and dealt with.' The propagator of unsound doctrine must be identified and put out of the fellowship (Rev. 2:14, 15, 20; II John 9, 10). But even here all is to be done with a view to eventual restoration on evidence of repentance and godly sorrow (II Cor. 7:8–12).

As in the nation so in the Christian congregations, there is an apparent lack of leadership. Scripture makes it plain that counsel must be given, wrongs have to be put right, care has to be provided. May the above study help to that end.

6

The Ministry of Women in the Church

OLIVE ROGERS

The Cultural Background to the Epistles

When in Old Delhi once, I visited the golden domed temple of the Sikhs. Being a woman, I was taken round to a back entrance and then through several rooms, till I reached the upper gallery where the ladies gathered. I sat on the richly carpeted floor and surveyed the scene. Suddenly, as so often in the East, the Scriptures became alive! We were high above the main body of the temple. The worship—intoning of the Sacred Book, and instructions for salvation—being carried on down below was pertinent only to the men, for they alone have souls to save. I tried in vain to hear what was going on, but the women were sitting around in groups gossiping, amused at the play of their children, careless of the fact that they were in a place of worship. For them a visit to the temple was merely an opportunity to escape from the monotony of an existence behind the four walls of their homes, where they reign supreme in their own quarters, but where their lives seldom encroach upon those of their men-folk, who do all the work involving contact with the outside world.

Not many months later I attended one of the Christian conventions held annually in S. India. Day after day thousands of men and women sat under the large leaf shelter. The men's section of the 'pandal' was quiet and orderly as they listened to the Word, taking notes with assiduous care. The women's half was another matter. All the children were there, restless, demanding and noisy, and many of the women were sitting in groups chattering.

The Eastern woman has always been sheltered and kept apart from the mainstream of life in the world, and she has not been encouraged to break from the security which such an existence afforded. She would wear a veil at all times (I Cor. 11:2–16). It denoted her recognition of the lordship of her husband and also gave her dignity and protection. Even in these days no man would presume to intrude upon the privacy of a woman shrouded in her 'burqa' or 'pallu'—the end of her sari pulled over her head. In orthodox Hindu or Muslim homes the women are still not allowed to go out freely; they are veiled, and when the men-folk approach, they sidle away quietly into the women's quarters to remain out of sight until called by their master.

A journey in an Indian train can be instructive in these matters. The 'Ladies Compartment' is completely shut off from the rest of the carriage. No matter how hot or airless, the door is closed and no man is permitted to enter other than a close relative of the ladies inside, who will bring all necessary food and drink to the compartment, and even he will remain no longer than is absolutely essential.

In the South Indian language which I speak, in common with other Eastern languages, there is no difference between the feminine and neuter gender. A woman is 'a thing', 'the thing in the kitchen', a thing to be sold for a price called a dowry, valued in terms of animals, land or money. She has no inherent rights; she is the sole property of her husband, or if he dies, of her male relatives including her son.

I have seen a woman, on the death of her husband, being taken outside a village fully shrouded. There she was stripped of her jewellery and her glory, for her head was shaved. From then on she may never again allow her hair to grow or leave her head uncovered. It is to her shame (I Cor. 11:6) till she die that she has become a widow. Remarriage is unthinkable; has she not caused the death of her husband? Again, I knew a woman who lived an adulterous life and refusing to heed reproof, she was taken by the elders and had her hair cropped, thus bringing upon herself public dishonour (I Cor. 11:6).

63

It is still considered in the East either a disgrace or a misfortune for a girl to remain unmarried. An unmarried life is incomprehensible to the Eastern mind, which cannot conceive a single person living in sexual purity. The unmarried women of earlier days were almost invariably 'devotees' of the gods, temple prostitutes who were usually lavishly adorned with jewels and often immodestly dressed.

In New Testament times the Jewish and Greek cultures both decreed that a woman was neither expected nor permitted to learn from the Holy Scriptures, and the concept of a woman teacher was inconceivable. This attitude held true in India until as recently as the last century, when Pandita Ramabai's father was outcaste for daring to teach his daughter the sacred Hindu Vedas.

It was against a background such as this that the apostles wrote to the early churches. And it helps us to understand what the Scripture teaches if we appreciate something of the customs which still prevail in the East where Christianity has not yet shed its enlightening rays in sufficient degree to dispel the darkness and bondage of heathenism.

Women in the Bible
Basically the problems which confronted the early church were no different from those which confront the church today. How much does contemporary society influence the conduct of the church? To what extent should the liberty of the believer in Christ be tempered by local custom in order to maintain a good witness?

This matter is discussed in I Corinthians 11, and it is as part of the whole that the role of the women in the church is considered. Chapter 14 and I Timothy 2 also touch upon the public ministry of women. Such portions of these chapters which deal with the women's role should not be wrested from their context, but need to be understood as an integral part of a wider subject.

To gain a balanced view of the Scriptures they should be interpreted not only against the background of historic cultures, but also in the light of

1. What the Bible as a whole says about this subject.
2. Christ's attitude to women.
3. The practice prevailing in the early Church.

1. In Old Testament times women enjoyed the same privileges as men in worship. Many sang in the temple choirs (I Chr. 25:5f; Neh. 7:67). Women also served in the tabernacle, and the same word *sābā* is used of their work as that of the Levites (Exod. 38:8; I Sam. 2:22). These may have been wives of Levites or, more probably, widows who had dedicated themselves to the service of the Lord.

(*a*) Anna worshipped and gave thanks publicly in the Temple (Luke 2:36–38).

(*b*) Miriam, who led the women in public praise, is specifically identified as a prophetess (Exod. 15:20; cf. Mic. 6:4).

(*c*) Deborah was not prevented from prophesying by the law, and what a graphic song of triumph she composed (Judg. chs. 4 and 5)!

(*d*) Hannah's inspired prayer is recorded for us in I Samuel 2.

(*e*) Huldah was acknowledged as the outstanding prophetic figure of her day. When King Josiah sent Hilkiah, the priest, and the elders to consult with her, the Lord revealed His will through her (II Kgs. 22:8–20). Both Miriam and Huldah were contemporaries of great prophets: viz. Moses and Jeremiah (cf. II Kgs. 22:3 with Jer. 1:2), which fact refutes the contention that women received the prophetic gift only in the absence of qualified men.

2. Christ's total attitude toward women showed His unreserved appreciation of them. This was in contrast to the normal custom of those days dictated as it was by Rabbinic standards.

(*a*) He recognized women as persons and accepted their gifts, being supported materially by a group of

65

women who accompanied Him on His tours assisting in the ministry (Luke 8:1–3; Mark 15:41; Matt. 27:55).

(*b*) The Sanhedrin taught 'indulge not in conversation with womankind',[1] but Christ broke all such racial, traditional and sexual barriers with impunity (John 4:27).

(*c*) He defied Jewish custom also in permitting Mary to 'sit at His feet and learn' in Rabbinic fashion—a privilege granted to men only. He commended her for this, and exhorted Martha to choose the better part (Luke 10:42).

(*d*) According to the law, both of those caught in the act of adultery should be put to death (Lev. 20:10). The Lord being impartial, exposed the injustice and hypocrisy of man as He forgave the woman (John 8:1–11).

(*e*) He entrusted women with the most crucial fact of redemptive history: they were to witness to the disciples of His resurrection. This is truly remarkable since women's testimony was not regarded as sufficient to establish a fact legally in those days. No wonder the disciples hesitated to believe (Luke 24:11)!

(*f*) In the economy of the East, a sister could be an acute liability; but Christ declared that giving up a sister for His sake constituted a privation that He Himself would recompense (Matt. 19:29). This was a most unusual precept for a man of His time, but such was the value He put upon women.

3. In the Early Church it is evident that women took as active a part as the men.

(*a*) The Spirit fell equally on men and women (Acts 2:1–4).

(*b*) The women prayed with the men (Acts 1:14; I Cor. 11:4f).

(c) There were women evangelists, co-workers with Paul (Phil. 4:2f).

(d) The Holy Spirit used women as well as men as His prophetic mouthpieces (Acts 21:9).

(e) Women taught in certain circumstances (Acts 18:26–28; II Tim. 1:5; 3:14f; Titus 2:3–5).

(f) There were deaconesses in the local churches (Rom. 16:1; I Tim. 3:11).

(g) Note the impressive list of women commended for their loyal service in Romans 16.

Thus it is clear that nowhere in Scripture is it indicated that women should be wholly silent. Prayer, praise and prophesying were permitted by the law and were also customary in the early church.

The Place of Women in the Epistles

There were however two opinions held concerning women in the church in ancient times just as there are today. At one extreme, there was an overlapping of the pagan attitude that a woman was inferior, the property of her husband. This produced an unnatural and improper subjection of women on the part of the men in the church. Many women were content to fill such a role. They were believers, but as women it did not occur to them that they should take seriously the matter of learning all they could about their new-found faith. Religion had always been the prerogative of the men, their place was in the home. At the other extreme, there were those women who were influential in their own spheres, some even owning their own businesses or properties. They realised that in Christ 'there is neither male nor female' (Gal. 3:28b) and that as believers they were equal with men in the sight of God. They thus found the restrictions of the heathen society irksome, especially the hampering veil, and they wished to cast it off.

The Apostle discusses this particular issue within a more wide-ranging discourse. I Corinthians 11 is a natural sequel to chapter 10. 'Why should my liberty be determined by another man's scruples?' (10:29). To this he replies, 'Give no offence to Jews, or to Greeks or to the church of God' (v. 32). 'Be imitators of me, as I am of Christ' (11:1). Here is the crux of the matter: in all things we should take Christ as our example. But what aspect of Christ's example does the Apostle encourage us to follow here?

For the purpose of bringing redemption to mankind, He who was equal with God, voluntarily became subject to the Father (Phil. 2:6). He did not act on His own initiative though He could well have done so, but willingly submitted to the authority of the Father (John 8:28, 42 etc.). Such was the complete oneness and interdependence of the Son with the Father, that Christ declared, 'The Son can do nothing of His own accord' (John 5:19). This was the practical submission of an equal for a specific purpose, and it in no way rendered Him inferior to or unequal with the Father.

This is the pattern for the woman. Equal as she is with the man, she will acknowledge his leadership within the church as being divinely ordained and inter-relate accordingly. This relationship in the days of the Apostle was expressed by the wearing of the veil. Thus in keeping with contemporary custom, the Apostle says that to wear the veil would avoid offence to both Jewish and Gentile communities. For believing women of those times to have discarded the veil would have created grave misapprehension as to the morals prevailing in the church, and this had to be avoided at all cost, especially in the licentious city of Corinth.

At the same time, Paul describes the veil in verse 10 as 'authority' upon her head. The Western mind finds this concept strange, that the wearing of the veil denotes *not the authority of the man over the woman but rather her own authority and power* within the divinely ordained hierarchy. Ramsay defines the Oriental view: 'Without the veil the woman is a thing of naught, whom anyone may insult. A woman's authority and dignity vanish with the discarded veil.' He suggests that the nearest equivalent we know is the 'authority' which a magistrate wears upon his head vesting him with power.[2]

The Apostle also implies that since the angels veil their faces in the presence of a thrice holy God, it would offend them to see the unbecoming familiarity and lack of reverence in an unveiled woman worshipper.[3] As H. L. Ellison comments, 'Every time and clime have had their expression of womanly modesty.' It hardly needs to be said however that the modern hat as worn in Western countries, almost only at church services, has little or no relation to the Eastern veil worn compulsorily at all times, for it carries neither the same significance nor performs the same function.

The Apostle next turns his attention to the men. Jewish men had been accustomed to wearing a head covering during worship. Now they are to discard it in recognition of the divine order, that under Christ the Head, they are appointed to authority in the church (I Cor. 11:7).

The injunction in I Corinthians 14:34 that women should keep silence in the church must be interpreted in the light of other Scriptures and should not be isolated from the other two references in the same chapter to keeping silence in the church (vv. 28, 30). The subject under discussion here is order in the church service. It may be clearly seen from Acts 1:14 and I Corinthians 11:4, 5 and I Timothy 2:9 that women are expected to pray and prophesy in the church meetings, albeit they are to be suitably attired. The silence imposed upon women here may not be taken as cancellation of a permission previously granted. It would be idle for the Apostle to prescribe dress when praying if, in fact, public prayer is denied to the ladies.

What then is the silence here? It should be remembered that there were no written New Testament Scriptures in the days of the Apostles, and discussion of the Old Testament Scriptures was an essential part of discovering the truths of their new faith (Acts 17:2, 17; 18:4, 19; 19:8f; 20:9 etc.). This was known as authoritative teaching, and much of it took the form of dialogue and debate. While it was conceded that women had the right, in fact the responsibility to learn, the apostle declared that they should not intrude into the debate of the teachers. The injunction to silence here is no contradiction of chapter 11. In point of fact, Paul is following the same principle. Once again he says that women, though spiritually equal with men, should cause no offence. They should follow the current practice. In those days girls did not attend public or synagogue schools. If they wished to do so, they learned at home from their brothers or fathers. In the same way, Paul says, women should learn at home from their husbands. For those of us who live in the East it is easy to imagine the dismay which would be caused if women were to call across from the ladies half of the congregation to their husbands sitting in the men's section. Such flagrant disregard of reverence in the presence of God would call forth a stern rebuke.

When Paul writes later to Timothy to give him instructions for the Ephesian church, he touches upon this subject again (I Tim. 2:8-15). Having stated that the women should be suitably attired when praying, he gives his reason why a woman is not permitted to teach or take authority in the church. It was when Eve stepped out of her position of dependence upon her husband and acted on her own initiative that she was deceived and sin entered. It was possibly to underline the danger of this in the church that Paul wrote 'yet woman will be saved through bearing children' (2:15). It seems that he was encouraging the Christian woman to realise that despite her new status as a person—with an eternal soul to save, of equal value in the sight of God, as much responsible for the use of the life with which God has endowed her as her male counterpart—she should not despise the traditional function of the woman. Child-bearing and rearing remain her primary calling, and as an enlightened believer she has a great responsibility to teach and train her children. For the unmarried there is a similar responsibility in the spiritual realm.

God's Divine Order

It would seem that were the divine order which God instituted in creation rightly understood and accepted many of our problems concerning the role of women in the church would cease to exist. Genesis 1:27 says so simply, 'So God created man in his own image, in the image of God he created him; male and female he created them.' Similarly Genesis 5:1 reads: 'When God created man, he made him in the likeness of God. Male and female he created them . . . and named them Man when they were created.' In these simple, uncomplicated statements we have the summation of our equality, the complementary nature and harmony of our humanity. We project the image of God as male and female, since God is male-female in His totality. It is necessary therefore to encompass both the male and the female in order to have a balanced projection of who God is.

In creation, God fully harmonized the sexes; and neither male nor female is complete without the other (I Cor. 11:11f). Thus Adam and Eve reigned together over God's creation as king and queen (Ps. 8:4–8). Together they fellowshipped with God, and they equally shared the blessings of God (Gen. 1:28). They were equally heirs of the grace of life together (I Pet. 3:7). Within this equality lies the authority-structure given by God. Man was created first, then the woman from the man and for the man. Thus man is the head (I Cor. 11:3). Small wonder is it that when sin entered, this most beautiful of all relationships, meant to display so perfectly the image of the Godhead and reflect the love of Christ for His church (Eph. 5:21–33), became the prime target of the enemy.

In Genesis 3:16 we see the results of the Fall. These are not the words of a harsh God pronouncing an unbearable penalty upon His disobedient children, but those of a God of infinite holy love announcing the inevitable and awful consequences of sin.[5] Man, God predicted, would take advantage of the weakness of woman, bringing a progressive domination over her until she would be reduced to a chattel, a mere 'thing', which is exactly what has pertained in non-Christian religions down the ages.

Christ's Work of Restoration
When Christ came, as we have been reminded, He restored

71

the dignity of the woman and gave to her, her rightful place in Society.

> In Christ once again she is equal with the man (Gal. 3:28b).
> In Christ she obtains salvation by faith exactly as the man does.
> In Christ her body becomes the temple of the Holy Spirit even as his.
> She is fed by the Word as he is.
> She may be the mouthpiece of the Holy Spirit as he also may be.
> She has access to the one common Father in prayer as he has, for she with him is ordained to the priesthood with all the responsibilities and privileges attendant upon such a high calling (I Pet. 2:9).

To limit public prayer to the men alone is to proclaim a doctrine of the priesthood of male believers, and to restrict prayer and prophesying to women's meetings alone is to presuppose an inequality which does not exist.

Scripture assures us that spiritual equality is God's intention, and this perspective never varies whether stated in the Old Testament or in the New. Paul in Ephesians 5:21f says, 'Be subject to one another out of reverence for Christ. Wives, be subject to your husbands, as to the Lord.' For practical purposes, within the equality which God has created, there must be a head. Thus, man as head, with Christ for his example, will take the initiative, not sparing himself. Woman, taking Christ also as her example, submits and co-operates; and her obedience becomes a joy, as both of them are activated by the love of Christ. Just as Christ is the glory of God, that is, the full expression of God, so the woman is the glory of man; she is a prepared complement to his maleness, and without her he is incomplete (I Cor. 11:7). Each is dependent upon and is necessary to the other. Mutual submission as a wider principle within the church is a spiritual commitment for which we are answerable to the Lord, 'for none of us lives to himself'.

The tragedy is that for many generations there has been an imbalance in our churches. As a result women generally have been content to remain inarticulate. Many are incapable of prayer in public, and even more serious, they are not able to communicate the truths of their Christian faith to others. And worse, they are not distressed that this is so. This means that a large section of each church has become atrophied, incapable of action, thus seriously hampering the effective witness of the church as a whole.

The steps which should be taken to rectify this position will inevitably vary from place to place and from time to time, but it seems incontrovertible that the women with their homes are the key to the evangelisation of today's unchurched peoples. They need to be given all the loving, gentle encouragement and stimulus that is possible to help them to overcome the inhibitions and fears of the years. The responsibility for this initiative lies with the elders of each local church, who with the deaconesses of their appointment, should make every effort to discover and develop latent gift among the women and thus bring about a total involvement of the church in realistic and effective outreach.

It is certain that if our eyes were open rightly to understand God's order for the church there would be less fear on the part of the men that their position of leadership and authority in the church was being challenged and less apprehension on the part of the women that their activities were being misconstrued. A family is complete and happy when both father and mother work in harmony, each filling his or her own God-appointed role efficiently. So the local church as a spiritual family will be really effective only when both men and women work side by side at the assignment for which each has been called and endowed.

NOTES

1 Louis M. Epstein, *Sex Laws and Customs in Judaism* (1942), pp. 107–19
2 W. M. Ramsay, *The Cities of St. Paul* (1907), pp. 203–5
3 F. F. Bruce, *An Expanded Paraphrase of the Epistles of Paul* (1965), p. 99, note
4 H. L. Ellison, *The Household Church* (1963), p. 86
5 Cf. H. L. Ellison, *The Message of the Old Testament* (1969), p. 20

7

The Church and The Family

JOHN R. WATSON

The Family under the Old Covenant

God's interest in the family is as old as the dawn of creation. The Genesis story immediately introduces us to family life and commends it with God's great declaration 'It is not good that the man should be alone; I will make him a helper fit for him' (Gen. 2:18). Thereafter we are swiftly introduced to the family lives of Adam, Noah and Abraham, which set the scene for two great principles about family life which are developed in the Pentateuch:

1. That God's covenant, first made with Abraham and later extended to the nation that grew out of his family, promised the blessings of God to the family and household of the man who obeyed God (Deut. 7:12, 13; 28:9–11). On the other hand, failure to obey the law of God would bring upon the disobedient disastrous judgement that would extend to his family and posterity (Deut. 28:15 et seq.).

2. That the family unit was God's appointed means of communicating the knowledge of His law to succeeding generations (Deut. 6:6–9). This principle is for ever enshrined in some of the wise sayings of Solomon. 'Train up a child in the way he should go, and when he is old he will not depart from it' (Prov. 22:6).

It is evident that the faithful in Israel held closely to these two principles right down to our Lord's day and that family life had largely been moulded by them.[1]

74

Jesus and the Family

It was therefore entirely in keeping with the ways of God that the Son of God made man should be committed to the care of a humble yet devout Jewish family where the law was carefully observed (see Luke 2:22–24) and the children instructed in its teachings. Also, it was entirely fitting that the mystery of the eternal Godhead should be expressed to men in terms of the family relationship of Father and Son, and that the intimate fellowship of Christ and His church should be likened to the close family links between parents and children, brothers and sisters (for example, Rom. 8:14–17; Heb. 2:11; Jas. 2:14–16).

The public ministry of the Son of God was completely consistent with all that God had revealed to Israel about the place of the family in the nation of God. In all the burdens that weighed upon His soul in His final three and a half years of ceaseless work He was constantly mindful of the privileges and responsibilities of both parents and children. He Himself accepted the household of Joseph and Mary as His own family, accepting Joseph as if he were His father (Luke 2:48) and the other children as His brothers and sisters (Matt. 13:55, 56). His references to the sacred tie of marriage (for example, Matt. 19:3–9), to fathers and to children (for example, Matt. 7:9–11), all show that He accepted the family as God's normal human unit. He only envisaged its unity being rightly broken when challenged by the supreme loyalty to Himself (Matt. 10:34–39). Likewise, His actions paid tribute to the Divine institution of the family as, for example, His sharing in the family fellowship of the home at Bethany (Luke 10:38–42) and His tenderness with Jairus (Luke 8:41 ff.) and the widow of Nain (Luke 7:11–15) when bereaved of their children.

When the church of our Lord Jesus Christ was established, founded upon His atoning sacrifice upon the cross, the foundations were laid by God's appointed men, the apostles (Eph. 2:20; 3:5). Their teaching, preserved for us in the epistles of Paul and other apostles, reveals that Christ's purpose for the family within His church is entirely con-

sistent with the law of Moses and with the teaching of Christ
Himself. Four principles regarding the family are laid down
in the epistles which are our chief guide as to the structure
and witness of the church.

1. The Epistles underline the Lord's endorsement of the
sanctity of marriage, amplifying His teaching to show that
marriage in the mind of God was an inviolable union
between a man and a woman both of whom are 'in the Lord'
(I Cor. 7:39; II Cor. 6:14). Paul however reflects the
tenderness of his Master towards Christians with unbelieving
marriage partners and makes it clear that such unions should
normally remain unbroken and also that the unbelieving
partner and the children are consecrated through the believing partner rather than the other way round (I Cor. 7:12–
16).

2. The Epistles however build considerably upon the basic
teaching that marriage within the church should be a
permanent union between believers. It raises such a union to
a partnership of love, in which each partner loves the other
with the same kind of selfless and sacrificial love that Christ
had when He gave Himself up as a sacrifice for the church
(Eph. 5:21–33). Peter speaks of the Christian man and wife
as 'joint heirs of the grace of life' exercising a united ministry
of prayer that will be hindered if the man acts inconsiderately
toward his wife (I Pet. 3:7). It is clear that Christian
marriage, which is the basis of family life within the church,
must be a partnership of love, not based on the dominance of
either husband or wife, but on the selfless devotion of each to
the other according to the supreme pattern of Christ.

3. It follows that the children of such a marriage between
Christians are born into an atmosphere of loving goodness
that should be parallel to that in the local church. In such a
helpful home a specific responsibility rests upon the Christian
father (as head of the marriage partnership) to teach his
children the truth of Jesus Christ. This is referred to in
Ephesians 6:4 as discipline and instruction, which we may
equate respectively with righteous standards and the doctrine
of the person and work of Christ. Men who have successfully

carried out this responsibility and thus managed their house-
holds well have given one indication of their fitness to carry
the responsibility of an elder or deacon (I Tim. 3:4, 5, 12;
Titus 1:6). It might be said that leadership of a Christian
family is regarded as a training ground for leadership in the
local church (I Tim. 3:5).

4. A further aspect of Christian family life that arises out
of Christian marriage is hospitality. Peter enjoins his readers
to 'practise hospitality ungrudgingly to one another' (I Pet.
4:9), regarding it as one way in which Christians can share
the grace which God bestows upon the individual (I Pet.
4:10, 11). Paul and John both encourage members of the
local church to be hospitable (Rom. 12:13; III John 5), John
seeing it as of special service towards servants of Christ who
have left their own homes to do God's service.

The Christian family and the Local Church

It is not difficult to see from these basic principles various
ways in which the Christian family should contribute to the
well-being and the work of the local church, always provided
that it is closely identified with and integrated into it as
envisaged in New Testament references to the Christian
family. This contribution would appear to be along three
lines.

1. *In the pastoral ministry of the church.* The care of believers
of all ages is primarily a responsibility of the elders of the
church (I Pet. 5:1–4), but far too often time and pressure of
other responsibilities cause such ministry to be neglected. A
Christian family presided over by a father and mother who
are sensitive to the opportunities will often supply a pastoral
need that cannot otherwise be met. The atmosphere of a
home where Christ is the unseen Head will draw Christians
in need and enable them to share problems that might not be
made known to the church in other ways. The combined
wisdom and gentleness of a dedicated couple willing to give
time and prayer to individuals will often bring solace and
direction to troubled Christians.

Such counselling in the home should be undertaken as part

of the ministry of the local church and should never be at variance with the aims and principles for which the church stands. Ideally such a ministry should be recognized and encouraged by the leadership of the church, perhaps by recognizing the father of the household as an elder or deacon of the church.

2. *In the evangelistic testimony of the church.* The local church is failing in its responsibility if the gospel of Christ is not being made known in its locality. In days when so few can be persuaded to hear the gospel preached and the power of the printed page is comparatively small, the Christian home is still a powerful instrument of witness, as it probably was in Antioch, where the first Gentile church sprang up (Acts 11:19-21).

The well-ordered home, especially a Christian home, is still a very attractive setting for social contacts; and it is not difficult for most families to find frequent occasions for entertaining neighbours. Such occasions which may be for whole families, for parents, for young people or for children need not necessarily be directly evangelistic but occasions when neighbours are welcomed for their own sakes with the prayer that the Lord will give natural openings for making known God's love in Christ. Such initial contacts may, of course, lead to occasions when specific questions about the Christian faith are answered by simple statements of spiritual truth; these occasions may lead, in turn, to personal counselling or to attendance at an appropriate service or special meeting at the local church.

True neighbourliness will give other openings too, especially at times of special joy or crisis, when an appropriate loving action can open the door to a presentation of the love of Christ. In this way the word of the gospel is backed by the conviction of a personality that reflects Jesus Christ and is not simply in word only. To use John's words, we shall be loving not in word or in speech but in deed and in truth (I John 3:18).

3. *In the teaching ministry of the church.* Although this is, in the first place, the work of those raised up to minister the

word publicly in a particular church, the needs of individuals are so varied and complex that it is the duty of every experienced and established Christian to supplement the public ministry by amplifying and explaining in personal conversation points of difficulty met by individuals, especially those who are new believers. What better environment for such supporting ministry than in the loving atmosphere of a Christian home where devoted partners are happy to give time to a puzzled Christian who wishes to talk over some point of Christian doctrine or practice. In this we have been given the example of Priscilla and Aquila (Acts 18:24–28).

Such ministry will usually begin within the family circle on those occasions when the father gathers the whole family together to read the Scriptures and pray, but such family devotions will soon lead to a larger ministry of God's word if the home is an open and welcoming place for those not blessed with a happy home life.

Once again, such ministry in the home should be carried on in complete harmony with the responsible church leadership and should never become in any sense an alternative to the regular public ministry. The guiding principle should be to keep the unity of the Spirit in the bond of peace (Eph. 4:3).

Happy is the church that has the faithful and wholehearted support of several Christian families! If the testimony of such homes is fully in accord with the testimony of the church, they will contribute great strength and stability to the life of that church. But what contribution has the church to offer to the family?

1. *Teaching Christian standards of marriage and family life.* There is one paramount responsibility that the local church must bear towards the family in every age and in our own more particularly. It is to uphold the Christian standards of marriage and family life that have already been set out in this chapter. These standards need to be constantly taught in public ministry and in private counselling, as well as shown in daily life by those who are leaders in the local church (Titus 1:5–11; 2:3–5). Standards need to be set and in-

struction needs to be given to the young from their earliest days, since altogether different standards will quickly be advocated to the growing mind through the powerful media of this age.

But let all teaching regarding marriage and family life be with compassion, for there will be many whose lives have been spoiled by deviation from God's standards to whom the church must minister comfort and strength. As Peter writes, immediately after dealing with the subject of Christian marriage, 'Have unity of spirit, sympathy, love of the brethren, a tender heart and a humble mind' (I Pet. 3:8).

2. *Providing opportunities for family worship.* There are also spheres where the local church can offer help and encouragement to families to live according to the divine pattern. The church should always welcome Christian families who wish to worship together either at the Lord's Table or at some other regular service of worship, showing understanding for their needs because of the abiding influence of early contacts upon the children of the family. The length of these times of worship, the prayers, the hymns, the scripture reading and ministry should take some cognisance of the fact that children with Christian parents are present. Much they will not understand, but what they do take in will be the raw material of their minds upon which the parents will work in the quietness of the home.

There will be many families however whose needs will not be met by being welcomed at a regular service of worship. Some children are too restless to be absorbed by adult forms of worship; some families prefer the worship and teaching to be well within the reach of the child's comprehension; some families not committed to the faith will be prepared to attend a service. These facts need to be recognised by the local church by the provision of a family service to which whole families may come to worship and to hear God's word in a manner which takes into account the needs of younger children. In addition to providing a spiritual focus for the family, such a service may prove to be a vital arm of evangelism.

Public services are not however the only responsibility that the church has for the family, for there are individual needs that can never be met in that way. There must be a readiness to provide Christian counsel and advice for parents and children whenever this is needed and also a recognition of those who are best qualified to undertake each particular assignment. When family crises occur affecting individual Christians the local church must be ready to minister with faithfulness and understanding.

3. *Provision for special groups and needs.* Many needs of particular members of the family call for regular provision by the local church. Each church must know the Lord's will in such special directions, since no activity should divert it from its role of being a loving fellowship of believers of all ages. One regular commitment should be to arrange classes of instruction for young believers, for these classes will not only supplement any teaching given within the family circle but will also be evidence to the church of the personal faith of the young person who has not hitherto made an open commitment.

There will also be other special needs of the family which can be met by groups or societies within the church, such as men's meetings, wives' groups, and occasions specially geared to the needs of young people and children of various age groups. These will provide fruitful activity outside the home and, more often than not, bring opportunities for evangelism. Care, however, needs to be taken to prevent such groups from becoming exclusive or self-sufficient. Representative leaders of such groups should be represented among the elders and deacons of the church to ensure that their specialist work is an integral part of the church.

Happy is the church which ministers Christ to its families and whose families serve Christ in that same church with undivided loyalty. Such a church will grow in strength and will shine as a cluster of lights in a dark world (Phil. 2:14, 15).

NOTES

1 Alfred Edersheim, *The Life and Times of Jesus the Messiah* 1 (1886), p. 227

8

Christian Stewardship and Church Finance

A. Christian Stewardship:
Its Responsibilities and Privileges

ARTHUR T. GINNINGS

Will man rob God? Yet you are robbing me. But you say, 'How are we robbing thee?' In your tithes and offerings. You are cursed with a curse, for you are robbing me; the whole nation of you. Bring the full tithes into the storehouse, that there may be food in my house; and thereby put me to the test, says the Lord of hosts, if I will not open the windows of heaven for you and pour down for you an overflowing blessing (Malachi 3:8–10).

It is often felt, and sometimes suggested, that the Christian pathway would be easier to follow if it were more clearly signposted and fenced-in. And, in practice, it seems that some folk carry that sort of desire into effect by setting up signposts and fences of their own choosing, sometimes claiming for their personal *preferences* the status of *principles* which others should also recognize and adopt. The validity of any such claim is easily tested, however, by the application of two criteria, namely: Is it Biblical? *and* Is it relevant?

Divine Standards
In some respects, it must be admitted, there is less anxiety and stress in behaving as we are told to behave than in having to decide for ourselves how to behave in any particular situation. As every teenager discovers, it may be irksome to submit to the authority of others but it is even harder to accept responsibility for the consequences of one's

own decisions. That, of course, was the position in which God's people, the Israelites, found themselves under the Old Covenant, whereby every detail of their lives—personal, social and religious—was governed by the Law given to them by God through His servant Moses (Exod. 20:1–17). Every Israelite could test his intentions and behaviour against the pronouncements of that code and thereby know at once whether and, if so, to what extent he/she was falling short of divine standards. Those standards were, and still are, the basis on which man can achieve his best in all aspects of life—rather like the maker's instructions supplied with an electrical appliance to ensure that it is maintained in good working order and operated at maximum efficiency.

On the other hand, the Devil's insinuations in the garden of Eden have been re-phrased in one form or another down the ages to suggest, in effect, that divine moral law was imposed on man to limit what he could become and achieve if permitted to develop and express himself totally as prompted by his natural instincts and aspirations. Thus human history is mainly a commentary on what has been achieved as the result of man's self-motivated endeavours and the record speaks for itself. Whereas many of his discoveries and inventions have been beneficial by any standards, man has failed to solve most of his own basic problems. Left alone, without access to resources outside himself, man has shown himself less capable of managing his own affairs successfully than he would want to admit. And, because of his unwillingness to accept personal responsibility, he blames anyone or anything else he can think of for the state in which he finds himself.

Now, against the background of God's moral law, the purpose of the present chapter is to examine the teaching and guidance in the Bible with reference to the responsibility of every child of God to account for and to return to God the due proportion of what has been freely received from Him. The time at our disposal, the skills we have acquired, the treasure we have accumulated, are all directly or indirectly derived from God's free gifts of life, health, strength, intelligence and personality. Furthermore, the sources of our food, clothing and shelter are also made freely available as supplied by God—it is the 'middlemen' who make them expensive!

Under the Law, God's people were required to set apart a specified day each week in order to rest from their otherwise normal activities in order to devote themselves to divine worship and service (Exod. 20:8–11). Mathematically, this meant the allocation of about fourteen per cent of their time for such activities, apart from the other special occasions when particular events were celebrated. As to their treasure (wealth) they were duty-bound to give a minimum 'tithe' (Lev. 27:30–32) or ten per cent; and, in addition, those who could do so were encouraged to give more as a 'free-will offering' (Lev. 22:17–25). As to their talents, the Old Testament record is liberally sprinkled with examples of men and women whose leadership, craftsmanship, priesthood, public administration and other skills were used for the glory of God and the blessing of His people.

It was within that framework that the life-style of the Israelites was regulated, despite many traumatic changes in other respects, for some twelve hundred years under the Old Covenant, until the coming of their Messiah in the person of the Lord Jesus Christ. In fact, those who refused to accept Him as the Messiah, and those who still refuse to do so, are supposed to maintain that life-style until, as they believe, the 'true' Messiah appears in due course.

New Testament Principles
As the New Testament makes abundantly clear, however, the coming of Jesus Christ and His life and work are the fulfilment of all the Old Testament predictions concerning the Messiah (Gal. 3:23–4:7). And one of the important things related to that coming was the establishment of His church under a 'new covenant' which did not destroy the old one (Matt. 5:17–20) but replaced it by something better (Heb. 8:6–13). Now, instead of being governed by a code of rules and regulations, God's people are provided with the Word of

God (the Bible) and the Holy Spirit (the Interpreter) to guide them in every possible combination of circumstances at any time and in any place.

Relating this principle to the purpose of the present chapter, it is interesting to observe how this led members of the early churches in Jerusalem and elsewhere to pool their resources to the extent necessary to ensure that the basic activities of the group were maintained, that poverty within (and to some extent beyond) the group was relieved, and that individuals who gave their time to ministering to the needs of others were supported to the extent that they could not support themselves by engaging in gainful work. This state of affairs has been referred to as 'Christian communism'—which, although not an inaccurate description is, possibly, in danger of being misunderstood. The basic principle, it seems, is expressed in the phrases 'they had everything in common' (Acts 4:32) and 'distribution was made to each according to his need' (4:35). No one was compelled to put the whole of his/her possessions into the common pool; what was so pooled was given voluntarily under the prompting and guidance of the Holy Spirit, with the result that 'there was not a needy person among them' (4:34). The fundamental differences between the doctrine of the 'common life' of the church on the one hand and the ideologies of humanistic communism on the other need not be discussed here. The child of God under the new covenant, growing by grace into spiritual maturity (Eph. 4:11–16), will be aware of a spirit-motivated desire to give to God as a free-will offering at least as much as others who are compelled by legal requirements or enthused by ideological objectives give to *their* gods.

Our Lord clearly taught in relation to the parables of the 'talents' (Matt. 25:14–30) and the 'pounds' (Luke 19:11–26) that every individual is a trustee of what he/she has been given by God, and is accountable to Him for the way in which such gifts are used or neglected. Extending that principle, the New Testament is full of exhortations with the common purpose of encouraging every child of God to discover, develop and demonstrate the gifts so given and received (I Tim. 4:14–16; II Tim. 1:6–7). Initially, for each person, that process is assisted by the teaching of Scripture and the example of others; subsequently, it flows on from each such person as a blessing to others and thus the cycle is repeated from one generation to another.

It has been possible only to mention in outline some of the principles taught in the New Testament about giving against the background of the Old Testament. Hopefully, enough has been stated to indicate how God's people can and should be guided about their giving under the new (second) covenant of grace. Our response could be no better expressed than by the well-known words of the hymn by Sylvanus Dryden Phelps (1816–1895):

> Saviour! Thy dying love Thou gavest me;
> Nor should I aught withhold, my Lord, from Thee;
> In love my soul would bow, my heart fulfil its vow,
> Some off'ring bring Thee now, something for Thee.

> All that I am and have—Thy gifts so free—
> In joy, in grief, through life, O Lord for Thee!
> And when Thy face I see my ransomed soul shall be
> Through all eternity something for Thee.

Practical Guidelines

Before concluding, it may be helpful to make one or two observations about the practical implementation of Christian giving. First, in common with the successful management of any project, the first element to be considered is *planning*. Most people can, with hindsight, see how by better planning they could have achieved more by the expenditure of less time, effort, expense, anxiety, and so forth, in the past. Too late, often, it is realised that *planned giving leads to ordered living*. Another point is that, subject to over-riding limitations, planning should be on a long-term basis but subject to short-term reviews. In doing so, it should be recognized that circumstances change by the effects of accidental as well as natural events and developments and, consequently, the capacity for giving by any individual is likely to vary in kind as well as in real and relative terms at various stages of life. At one stage, the major element in one's giving may be time and/or skill; at another stage it may be in terms of money and/or advice. By understanding this it is easier to accept the fact that one is no longer able to do what one could.

The poor widow (Mark 12:41–44) was commended by the Lord—not so much for what she gave in *real* terms but because in *relative* terms she gave more than others who, in real terms, had given more: 'she out of her poverty has put in everything she had'. On another occasion, in different circumstances, He accepted a gift from one of whom He said: 'She has done a beautiful thing to me. . . . She has done what she could' (Mark 14:1–9). Later still, Peter was not ashamed to admit that he was penniless when asked for alms, but he had something better to give than money: 'I have no silver and gold, but I give you what I have; in the name of Jesus Christ of Nazareth, walk' (Acts 3:6).

The second element to be mentioned is *covenanting*—in two senses, one general and the other technical. A covenant is, of course, another term for what is generally referred to as a contract. A contract is an agreement between any two persons (or groups) whereby certain goods and/or services are supplied by the one and paid for by the other—subject, generally, to conditions. The significance of this in relation to the 'old' and 'new' covenants between God and mankind does not need to be elaborated. It reminds us, however, that even as God has bound Himself by those covenants so also bound are those who enter into a covenant relationship with Him. Therefore, acknowledging that all we are and everything we have is directly or indirectly a gift from God, and recognizing the responsibility and privilege of every child of God to give back to Him a due proportion of what he possesses in terms of time, talent, and treasure, we should honestly and objectively assess our essential personal and dependent needs against our resources—with professional assistance if necessary; and, having done so, we can enter into a private and personal covenant with God to give what seems to be right and proper in the circumstances. By entering into such a covenant, many Christians have proved the faithfulness of God in the fulfilment of His promises or, so to speak, His part of the covenant (Mal. 3:10).

Then, too, in relation to the giving of money, the term *covenanting* has another and more technical significance for residents in those countries such as the United Kingdom whose fiscal regulations permit the State to refund the amount of income tax paid by individuals on the sums they give to charitable objects under a formal Deed of Covenant for a period not less than seven years. At the rates in force at the time of writing, United Kingdom tax-payers can thereby make available for the Lord's work about half as much again as they give directly. It is therefore surprising that more, if not all, Christian tax-payers do not take advantage of this provision. Some, at least, may be unaware of this facility and/or what is involved in making use of it. Others, meaning to do something about it, have not implemented their intentions—yet.

Another group consists of those who fear that they may not be able to keep up their payments over a period as long as seven years and/or do not feel clear about committing themselves to the support of a particular organisation or ministry for that length of time. Another sort of resistance is based on the (specious) grounds that 'covenanting' is a back-door method by which secular money (the State's) is being acquired to support the Lord's work. All such fears and objections can be answered and enquiries would be welcomed by various Christian agencies which have been set up to offer service and advice in this regard.[2]

'All right,' says someone, 'I realise that as a Christian I have a responsibility to "give"; I will work out conscientiously how much I ought to give regularly and systematically. But then, having done that, where/how/when should I give it?' And that sort of question takes us back to the beginning of the chapter. Today, every Christian can and should seek his/her guidance for all decision making by setting the questions to be answered against the Word of God and submitting himself to the promptings of the Holy Spirit.

'But then,' says the questioner, 'how can I distinguish between the promptings of the Holy Spirit and my own inclinations?' Such distinction is not necessary unless there is conflict, and there never will be conflict between the Word and the Spirit. Furthermore, the guidance thus received is seldom (perhaps never) given unilaterally in the sense that it fails to find accord with others whose guidance is received by the same means. In particular, the counsel of experienced fellow Christians can be a further source of help in making decisions about giving as well as about many other matters.

The Ultimate Test

Finally, and above all, let us appreciate that, to be truly effective, our giving must begin with ourselves. Our supreme example in this, as in all else, is our Saviour and Lord (Phil. 2;5–7; II Cor. 8:9); that example was followed by many of His followers including members of the early churches in Macedonia (II Cor. 8:1–5). It is according to our faith and our faithfulness that we are judged: 'This is how one should regard us, as servants of Christ and stewards of the mysteries of God. Moreover, it is required of stewards that they be found trustworthy' (I Cor. 4:1–2). We are not concerned about the yardsticks by which success is measured in other quarters; it is within the reach of every Christian to merit our Lord's commendation: 'Well done, good and faithful servant; . . . enter into the joy of your master' (Matt. 25:21, 23).

NOTES

1 Please read II Corinthians 8:1–9:15 as a background to the subject of this chapter

2 There are Christian trusts who would be glad to give advice or assistance in the area of stewardship such as: The Macedonian (Evangelical) Trust, North Staffordshire Evangelical Trust, U.K. Evangelical Trust (Inc.), and others

B. Church Finance:
An American Experience

DONALD M TAYLOR

Speaking at a conference on the west coast of America, a pioneer preacher was telling how he erected church buildings in a Maritime province on Canada's east coast. 'I looked to the Lord for the necessary funds, not to Stewards Foundation, and with my own hands did the building,' he said. A trustee of the Foundation in the audience, who was thoroughly enjoying the pioneer's report, later had opportunity to entertain him, but carefully avoided all reference to the subject of church financing from the ground up.

But later in the midwest, without naming the worker, he mentioned the incident to a man who also had spent years in the Maritimes. 'I know the man,' said this worker. Although a rather isolated individualist, he was doing a good work; but, to the mind of my informant, he was failing to use the excellent opportunity of the erection of a suitable meeting place to instruct his converts in giving to the Lord for His work. By borrowing on mortgage from Stewards Foundation or some local financing source, they would be faced with the responsibility of meeting monthly payments. Thereby they would be made aware that the church, with its head in heaven, carrying on its work in this world in buildings made with hands and with other material means, is expected to move along on the dedicated labour and contributions of its members.

Gradually, under wise leadership, these converts would learn to give systematically, regularly, to the furtherance of the gospel, the needs of their own local church for maintenance, for outreach through Sunday school, evangelistic campaigns, to foreign missions, and the like. They would begin to realize that the man who brought the gospel to them and then brought them to faith in the Lord Jesus Christ was not supported with pennies rained down from heaven, but

90

through monetary gifts given by individuals and churches. In short, they would learn that they had the privilege and responsibility of sharing what the Lord was providing for them through their employment and other avenues for the furtherance of His work and the glory of His name.

A Pioneer Venture

The experience of Stewards Foundation in North America and the signal evidence of the Lord's blessing on its ministries may be an encouragement to Christians in other countries. W. G. McCartney of Chicago, confronted with the financing of a new church building, and finding commercial lending institutions, such as banks, generally unwilling to lend to churches for various reasons—one purpose buildings, poor financial risks, and fear of adverse publicity if they should have to foreclose on a church mortgage—began to think about a central agency that could borrow from Christians and lend to individual assemblies as the need arose. Four other men joined with him in setting up a non-profit corporation, and the work began. The charter embraced the financing of church building (purchase, remodelling, expansion), camps and conference grounds, homes for elderly Christians and for children, hospitals and Bible schools. From its inception loans were made to Canadian as well as American (U.S.) church and camp projects, conference grounds and homes. In time, because of fluctuations in exchange rates, it was found advisable to set up a Stewards Foundation (Ontario) for Canada and, to the extent feasible, separate the financial work of the two organizations, while carrying on their operations from the same office.

Bonds of a variety of denominations and of maturities and rates of interest were issued to lenders, and, with some rare exceptions on very small loans, mortgages were required of borrowers. Needs for assembly-related financing outside Canada and the United States in a relatively few instances were met with the requirement of United States or Canadian guarantors. In time we learned that some who readily signed as guarantors were horrified when faced with the prospect of making good their guaranties. So future loans for overseas missionary work were made to home churches, who in turn passed the money on to the missions, missionaries and assemblies in other lands. The responsibility for repayment rested in the homelands.

One country which has a large number of assemblies in its chief city with a number of well-to-do members frequently asked for Stewards Foundation loans. When offered help to set up their own foundation for financing their church-related projects, they declined. Those who could have bought bonds to provide financing within their own country felt they could not afford to do so, as they could get so much higher interest from other investments. That is not the whole story, of course. The well-to-do often are not in the churches that require financing. Fluctuation in exchange rate and in international relations makes it impractical to lend United States or Canadian dollars. However, assembly leaders in two other countries have with counsel from Stewards Foundation set up their own financing organizations.

Since inception Stewards Foundation and Stewards Foundation (Ontario) have financed some 700 church building, remodelling and expansion projects, youth camps, Bible conference grounds, Christian homes for elderly Christians and for children, Bible schools, hospitals and nursing homes in North America. It operates five hospitals (three of them in affiliated corporations), all with Christian administrators and chaplains and open to the general public. These have been able to provide care without charge to many missionaries and home workers, as well as scholarships for students in medicine and nursing.

The diligent work of the chaplain and the administrator of one of these hospitals in a small city on the west coast of America has resulted in the recent development of a local church, which already has commended two missionaries to foreign fields. In all the hospitals, not only the chaplains but other Christians employed there carry the gospel to patients, visitors and other employees, along with comfort to Christian patients. Obviously, good care of the sick is essential to effective Christian work in these institutions. All of them are regularly accredited by the Joint Commission on Accreditation of Hospitals, which at regular intervals meticulously inspects for quality of care. The administrator and the chaplain of another of the west coast hospitals were chiefly instrumental in the planting of another flourishing assembly. In each instance a major part of the financing for the chapel came from Stewards Foundation.

Years of experience with many assemblies has shown that in general not more than twenty-five to thirty per cent of income should be applied to debt service. Operational expenses, including honoraria for speakers and gifts to home and foreign missionaries, will take the balance of income.

The Support of Workers

Few assemblies of Brethren, to our knowledge, support in full the workers commended by them to home and foreign fields; although those who have a preacher, teacher or personal worker who devotes all his labour to work in and around the local church normally feel responsible for his entire support. There is a slow but steadily growing tendency for gifted speakers and personal workers and pastors to devote the major part of their labours to one church and its immediate neighbourhood. Consequently, support comes from that church and its individual members. In Canada and the United States itineration is more and more being limited to those who have a definite, recognized gift for teaching and evangelism and to missionaries on furlough. In most areas one-church-based evangelistic campaigns are a thing of the past. (I must refrain from commenting on the merits or demerits of this trend.) Larger campaigns with men who devote their full time to evangelism are the order, with many and sometimes all evangelical churches in the community or an even wider area cooperating. This spreads the quite substantial cost of the campaign over a wide contribution base. However, a few months before this writing, a single California church brought a well-known evangelist from England for a week of meetings, for which they rented a building in their area much larger than their own chapel. They felt the visible results justified the expenditure of time, effort and money.

Summer conferences for Christians provide excellent ministry in a vacation atmosphere and enable the speakers to talk to a large group of believers on a portion of Scripture over a week or more. The speakers, it is assumed, are usually adequately remunerated for their ministry and expense of travel. Yet those individuals who comprise the audience are not overburdened with the fairly substantial expense, as it is shared equally among all. Again, tape cassettes made from recordings at such conferences will carry such high quality ministry to individual Christians unable to attend and to assemblies that cannot find comparable ministry in their area for midweek meetings. Also studio recorded series of messages by competent expositors are available for nominal cost. Thoughtful assemblies will make some financial acknowledgement to the speakers when they use their addresses in this way.

Practical Guidelines

At the time Stewards Foundation began financing assembly and assembly related projects in North America the general practice for assemblies was to make no provision for future building or expansion needs. Some few probably thought it unscriptural to lay up funds for future needs, while others, dispersing dollars as soon as they came in, blithely assumed that the money would be there when they needed it. Building funds were a rarity. Now many a local church sends money sporadically or regularly to the Foundation for the purchase of Bonds that earn interest or otherwise invest money locally in order to make provision for anticipated remodelling, expansion, or a new building in another location.

Personally, I suggest that every church should have a committee to keep an eye on the changing character of its geographical location so that the church will not suddenly wake up one day to find that it is performing no useful mission in the area, that its congregation has dispersed to outlying districts, and that the area for various reasons is no longer suitable as a location for their church building. This has happened over and over again, resulting in obsolescence and hence waste of the money often sacrificially given for the work of the Lord.

Every commercial lending institution is concerned as to the degree of involvement of the borrower in his proposed project. And a prime measure of this is the percentage of the total cost the borrower is advancing. Also, the lender wants to know what the prospects are of maintaining regular payments on the loan. In the interest not only of those Christians and churches who entrust their savings to it, but also of the borrowing assembly or assembly group, an organization such as Stewards Foundation must delve into the borrowers' financial affairs. So its application forms ask pertinent questions concerning assets, liabilities, funds set for the project, average of regular offerings and other income, and whether all in the church, or at least a substantial majority, favour the project. It also wants to know if the trustees or other responsible brethren are willing to insure repayment of the loan. It delves into building costs, and usually makes an on-the-spot review of the project with one or more of the elders of the local church. It requires mortgage or trust deed papers and proper title guarantee. In consequence, when the loan is made it is on a sound footing and very frequently the local elders have learned a great deal about financial affairs. They realize their responsibility. Also these on-the-spot checks save them from going overboard in building and protect them from unscrupulous bidders and contractors who are more eager than knowledgeable. With rare exceptions these loans call for monthly payments of one per cent per month or more; the amortization period varying in keeping with the prevailing interest rate. The Foundation has learned that interest rates well below the market may encourage borrowing for a project more than the borrower is able to repay. Such loans handicap rather than help.

It may well be that some Christians coming together in a new area may be so eager to get a church planted and established that they neglect the necessary spade work: the thorough teaching of converts, educating them as to the Lord's pattern for worship and fellowship, breaking of bread and community prayer, and other Christian responsibilities and privileges. They want to get a meeting place of their own immediately; and in the glow of a new and exciting enterprise they want to build big, they want to build a church building that will be an architectural asset to the neighbourhood. Sometimes these believers could well use a bit of the caution and waiting on the Lord of the pioneer preacher whose diatribe against Stewards Foundation and its ilk opened this chapter. He waited until enough free money came to him to start building. He was unconcerned—as he well could be in his unzoned, unrestricted area—about appearances. All he wanted was a shelter where the Word of God could be taught and the gospel preached. And this could be built for a few thousand dollars. Neighbours were not critical. His building was not unlike their own houses.

On the other hand, one cannot put up a shack in a zoned residential neighbourhood. Land is expensive. And if one were permitted to build too cheaply this would drive people away rather than induce them to come in. Thus patience is needed. It may be well to find one or more rooms in a local school or some other suitable building which could be used until a suitable building site is found at a reasonable cost. This would give time for sober thought as to size of building, facilities, Sunday school requirements, etc., and would allow for the storing up of some capital for the actual building.

Some assemblies save, initially at least, considerable interest by borrowing from their own membership. But in most cases the lenders of non-interest-bearing dollars will need their money back after a few years. They can then get financing to replace these dollars from local lending institutions or from the Foundation.

Doing the Lord's Work in a Business-like Manner
While it may well be possible to go overboard on financial matters to the detriment of the local church's primary

functions of preaching the gospel to the unsaved and building up believers, there is no scriptural reason for doing, or trying to do, the Lord's business in an unbusiness-like fashion. So it is well that by example and precept—the former being more effective than the latter—that the believers be taught to give generously. And this certainly can be backed up adequately by Scriptures, such as I Timothy 6:17–19, Exodus 25:1–8; 36:3–7; Acts 4:34–37; I Corinthians 16:1–4; II Corinthians 8 and 9; Philippians 4:14–19.

In some countries this giving for the work of the Lord, as for other charitable enterprises, is encouraged by the State. Perhaps the most generous of all nations in this matter is the United States, which now allows tax deductible giving up to fifty per cent of otherwise taxable income. So, for example, on a net taxable income of $20,000 a Christian can give up to $10,000, and thereby eliminate that amount from his taxable income. Thus, in effect, the state is sharing with him in his contributions, for the larger the percentage of tax-free giving the more he should be able to give for the Lord's work.

Through agencies such as Letters of Interest, Christian Missions in Many Lands, and his local church, he can make tax deductible gifts to missionaries and mission enterprises overseas. In Canada, where deductible gifts may constitute much less of taxable income (now up to twenty per cent), he can make his contributions through both his local church and Missionary Service Committee. Numerous contributions both of money and goods are made through Workers Together, an extremely alert organization of assembly sisters in America.

While there are fairly frequent calls for disaster relief to churches and individual believers in other lands, and occasional needs for contributions to meet the financial problems of believers and others in the home lands, there seems to be far less of this need for local sharing than in past years. A major reason probably is a more affluent society, and with this Social Security for the elderly and handicapped, unemployment and workmen's compensation insurance. Most of the workers engaged in preaching and teaching are on Social

Security, it is assumed, as are also other believers in the population. This of itself does not provide a very adequate income usually, but it certainly helps.

Some brethren, happily, are especially concerned about the needs of the widows of missionaries and home workers. The most recent *Directory of Commended Workers in the United States and Canada* lists 71 widows. The mortality pattern seems not to have changed much from Bible days. While now as then there are men who outlive their wives, as did Abraham (Sarah) and Jacob (Rachel and Leah), there are now in the church many widows, as there were in Elijah's day in Israel. In Christian retirement and nursing homes, as also in secular homes, the proportion of female to male usually runs three or four to one: 75/80 women for 25/20 men. The women in general are widows or spinsters. Here surely is a field for service to which the Lord, who has special care for widows and orphans (Ps. 146:9; I Tim. 3:3–16), would have us give compassionate heed.

Systematic Giving

There are two distinct phases to providing systematically for the Lord's work from one's personal income: (1) setting aside a definite, pre-determined portion or percentage of income; (2) waiting on the Lord as to the distribution of that money. The second need not mean a special, seemingly miraculous, message from heaven as to where or to whom to send funds— although with some believers evidently it does on occasions— any more than the recipient should expect to receive needed money in any other way than by a gift put in the hand or received by mail. But it does certainly require an intelligent study of the many needs that are brought to the donor's attention and prayer as to where funds should go for other than regular church, mission and other normal obligations.

While the sporadic, unsystematic giver, contributing occasionally and impulsively to urgent appeals, runs the risk of giving unwisely and sometimes where much of the contribution is absorbed by fund-raising and home-office expense, the thoughtful, systematic giver also runs a risk. He may contribute wisely and well, but rather automatically without much joy in his giving. He could hardly be labelled a 'hilarious giver' (II Cor. 9:7, margin). Still he does well, and in times of financial stress may happily find that he has available for the Lord's work some dollars when he has none for his own personal needs. That can give the joy akin to that of the poor widow who threw all her living into the treasury, while the observant Lord looked on unseen (Luke 21:2–3).

A Variety of Forms of Stewardship

A phase of stewardship or giving that is little recognized in the world in this money-conscious age is that of those who provide dedicated services for meagre wages or even for nothing. Yet the Christian woman or man who works diligently at a task for the Lord with little or no compensation may be giving far more than those whose generosity is heralded. Many a Christian has remained in a poorly-paying job rather than go where he could earn more and give more money, because he has a conviction that he is where the Lord wants him to be. And this does not apply only to Christian doctors, teachers and printers in mission fields, who could earn vastly greater income at home, but also to workers at home in nursing and retirement homes, and in other poorly paid occupations, who voluntarily contribute their talents and time for inadequate compensation.

Another form of Christian stewardship consists of turning money over to a church or school or other institution, and receiving in return a regular income for life. This was quite popular a few years ago when prices of things stayed fairly steady, and hence one knew fairly well what one's financial needs would be over the years. The trustee organization received a gift that on average far outweighed the value of the annuity, when a modest rate of interest was included. The donor received a dependable income for life. But today with wildly fluctuating currency values and cost of things rising constantly, annuities are poor investments.

It is estimated that about two-thirds of the general public, Christians included, fail to make any provision for disposition of the assets they leave behind. 'If any provide not for his own, and specially for those of his own house, he had denied the faith, and is worse than an infidel' (I Tim. 5:8), surely is as applicable to the disposition of one's estate at death as to caring for those for whom one is responsible while living. Good Christian stewardship then demands making provision while living for family members and relatives who may be left behind. This can be done by will or trust. And if one has developed an estate that is more than ample to meet his family obligations, there are many avenues by which he can channel the remainder into phases of the work of the Lord.

Good stewardship requires that the testator be as thoughtful concerning the distribution of his estate as he has been in accumulating it. If his estate is substantial he will need some expert help: a solicitor versed in estate matters and also a tax accountant. These persons can help him discern his responsibilities and desires and assist in drawing up the documents and plans.

Some years ago one Stewards Foundation related hospital received a bequest of $500 from a testator whose name they could connect in no way with the service of the hospital. He had not been a patient. He had not been an employee. The puzzled administrator at last learned from the lawyer who had drawn up the will that in discussing with the donor what disposition to make of his assets they had leafed through the telephone book's list of hospitals; connecting the name of the hospital with one commonly used by the denomination to which the testator belonged they had decided to list it among his beneficiaries. While the money was put to good use in the care of patients, and it was not a great sum, such disposition could hardly be classified as good stewardship. Yet far too often Christian people are even less thoughtful about the distribution of their estates. And in consequence there have been some very tragic happenings: wives have been left penniless when their spouses had every intention of providing amply for them; children who should have shared generously in an estate being disinherited because of widowers remarrying and making no provision for them; physically, mentally

67788

or emotionally handicapped relatives having no provision made for them, and so on.

One could go on and on about stewardship, but we will terminate this chapter with a final word that stems from a brief text, the word of our Lord Jesus Christ to two blind men who came to Him for sight: 'According to your faith be it unto you' (Matt. 9:29). The Christian who has confidence in the Lord's ability to provide for those near and dear to him, even as he has provided for them through his lifetime, will not be concerned as to their welfare whether he is able to leave them much or little. He will thoughtfully make such provision as is able to do, without stress or worry, and confidently lay their care in the Lord's hands, even as dying penniless, our Lord Jesus Christ laid the care of his mother in the hands of the beloved disciple.

9

The Church and World Mission

PAUL W MARSH

'One winter night I was talking with a shivering man slumped against a street lamp about the needs of his soul. A cold wind was blowing. Finally he turned to me and in the most pathetic way said, "Hey, look, friend, would you buy me a bowl of soup?" I had been warned not to give anything to these alcoholics. They would spend it on liquor. It did not occur to me that he was not asking for money. He was not asking for liquor. He wanted a bowl of warm soup in his stomach. He was cold and hungry.

'I said, "No! I've got something better to give you. I'm giving you Jesus Christ." He turned away with a disappointed look on his face and stood staring into the gutter while I talked about his soul. Finally he turned back a second time and said, "Hey, look, buddy, won't you buy me a bowl of soup?" And I said, "No! I'm trying to give you something better."

'How I wish I could live that day over! I would buy him ten bowls of soup. Here was a man in desperate physical need and I had no interest. How could I get through to his soul when he was standing there shivering, cold and hungry? I was talking about matters that held no interest for him at that moment. He wanted something warm in his stomach. That was the issue for him and I was not willing to face it. It would have cost only a few pence to buy him a bowl of soup and I could have done that. But I didn't.'

David Howard's experience on Chicago's Skid Row recorded in his book *How Come, God?* was no isolated event. It has been enacted with frightening frequency in a million corners of the world from the Thames Embankment in London to the body-strewn streets of Calcutta.

What is World Mission ?

Is it offering John 3:16 to a man or woman with an empty stomach, who probably has up to a dozen similarly empty stomachs lined up in the hovel he calls his home? Will it thrill him with gospel joy to know that 'man shall not live by bread alone'?

While it may be impossible to draw a clear line between 'straight evangelism' and mission, a distinction is evident. Man can too easily be viewed as a 'soul' to be saved, as if just one part of him had some particular significance to God. The fact that his Creator made him a total personality, with emotional, spiritual and physical needs, set in a physical environment, is frequently overlooked.

Mission, then, views man in the totality of his being, seeks to understand and meet him in the context of his total situation. Any concept of evangelism which ignores these factors will run into serious trouble. Neither is this a fact which is relevant only in some remote part of the globe. Failure in direct evangelism in Great Britain or North America—among the affluent as well as among the less privileged classes—is in many cases attributable to a faulty understanding of what mission is about.

Shireen Mohammed joins the queue at the mission clinic, and two-year-old Maqsud, limply straddling her hip, needs pills for the fever which refuses to break. The clinic, however, does not open yet; first, the 'good news' is given—not that the pills have arrived, but that Christ the Saviour has come. Is it good news to Shireen? Should she be forced, a captive audience, to swallow the gospel pill before she can get the other variety? The position can be defended: the good news and Christian compassion are presented, if not together, consecutively; it's the only way that a Christian contact can be made; some in such situations have come to Christ. Good, but other nagging questions remain: what of the numbers who resent—rightly?—their being cornered and forced to hear the Christian message; is it morally right to use medical work as a bait with which to hook men and women for Christ; does not medical work stand in its own right as a valid expression of the compassion of Christ, without strings attached?

Christ's compassion, and that of His followers, was frequently given without reserve or preconditions. Without overlooking the occasions when faith was called for, the instances when He healed solely because He had pity or compassion or saw a specific need, are significant. The widow of Nain and her dead son are a prime example (Luke 5:11–17).

The point to be demonstrated from the Skid Row situation, and the Asian scene, without in any way questioning the motives of those concerned, is that mission is larger than the verbal declaration of the terms of the gospel—larger, too, than demonstrations of Christian compassion and service which are so presented that the recipient is 'pressured' into the Christian position.

As is already obvious it is easy to be negative and destructive in an analysis of the Church's attitude to, and attempts at, mission. The glib attitude of 'preach the gospel, get people converted, and everything will fall into its proper place, with all problems solved', an attitude which has characterized much evangelical thought and activity, provokes such a reaction. Recognizing the faults of a superficial evangelicalism does not, however, entail the acceptance of a nebulous do-goodism which ignores the centrality of Jesus Christ in world mission. Without God in Christ there is no mission or good news for mankind.

In an occasional paper, *Viewpoint*, Jim Punton defines positively the nature of mission. 'The *source* of mission', he states, 'is God Himself. He is a sending God—sending His prophets, His Son, His Spirit, His people. . . . The *sphere* of mission is the "cosmos" the world. . . . God's mission is to restore the world to wholeness. . . . The *agent* of mission is Christ. . . . In Him the reign or kingdom of God is seen embodied and enacted; through His death and resurrection man can live within that reign now. The *message* of mission is good news of Jesus Christ—good news He brought and good news He is. . . . It is good news for the individual, good news for the world. It is *personal* and *social* and *global* and *cosmic*. Jesus is Lord!... The *scope* of mission is co-extensive with life. Your will be done on earth as in heaven. Is there an area of life which does not reflect God? Then mission extends there. "It is one of the essentials of the gospel that there should not be a single theme in this world which is not touched upon by the gospel."'

This statement is quoted at length since it can be sub-stantiated at every point by the biblical text: God as *source* through the prophets—'From the day that your fathers came out of the land of Egypt to this day, I have persistently sent all My servants the prophets to them, day after day' (Jer. 7:25); through His Son—'The Spirit of the Lord is upon me, because he has anointed me to preach good news to the poor. He has sent me to proclaim release to the captives and recovering of sight to the blind, to set at liberty those who are oppressed, to proclaim the acceptable year of the Lord' (Luke 4:18, 19; cf. John 3:17; 6:29); through His Spirit—'But the Counsellor, the Holy Spirit, whom the Father will send in my name, He will teach you all things, and bring to your remembrance all that I have said to you' (John 14:26); through His people—'Jesus said to them again, "Peace be with you. As the Father has sent Me, even so I send you" (John 20:21). The *sphere*: 'God so loved the world . . .' (John 3:16; cf. I John 4:9; II Cor. 5:19). The *agent*, Jesus Christ: 'But when the time had fully come, God sent forth His Son, born of woman, born under the law, to redeem those who were under the law, so that we might receive adoption as sons' (Gal. 4:45; cf. I John 4:14). The *message*: 'For I am not ashamed of the gospel: it is the power of God for salvation to every one who has faith, to the Jew first and also to the Greek' (Rom. 1:16). The *scope*: 'Thy kingdom come, Thy will be done, on earth as it is in heaven.' (Matt. 6:10).

This is world mission, not merely 'popping the gospel gun' and saving a soul, but the movement of God in Christ and out through the church, redeeming men and women as whole people and influencing every aspect of life. In these terms mission and evangelism cannot be separated; evangelism lies at the heart of mission.

Where is mission ?

The mere fact of travelling 7,000 miles never accomplished world mission nor made a missionary out of anyone. Mission is always where I am. John Wesley claimed the world as his parish; lesser mortals would do well to claim their road or street, their area of work or social involvement. Starting at the home base makes sense and may possibly lead on to more extensive outreach (cf. Acts 1:8). Jesus was enunciating a basic principle of world mission when He said to the healed demoniac, 'Go home to your friends, and tell them how much the Lord has done for you, and how He has had mercy on you' (Mark 5:19).

Although Britain and America have never been truly Christian, they have most certainly, with many other western countries, benefitted for centuries from the influence of Christianity and the Christian ethic. Historically, therefore, world mission has frequently been considered in terms which necessitated sending a Christian hundreds or thousands of miles from his home area. So arose the great missionary pioneers William Carey, Henry Martyn, Hudson Taylor, to mention only three. The great missionary societies and movements of independent churches were born, and Britain went to the world beyond.

The image of pith helmets, cholera belts and spine pads dies hard; but these have nothing to do with world mission today. The immense, trackless, unknown, mysterious and often romantic (till you get there) world far beyond the horizon, if not the imagination, has shrunk to MacLuhan's 'global village'. Barriers now exist not so much in physical terms, as in the areas of culture, prejudice, racialism, competing creeds and nationalistic aspirations.

Unevangelized areas abound and Christ's command remains (Matt. 28:19, 20). Yet the pattern of outreach is different: western missionaries no longer find themselves alone where once they followed the great trade routes to Asia or moved in behind the advances of western imperialistic expansion. Asia is awake, and the two areas of rapid growth are Africa and South America. While congregations shrink in Britain, they boom in Brazil; Africans are stirred for the needs of Africa, Asians for Asia. Missionaries continue to go overseas from the United Kingdom and North America in considerable numbers, but they often work alongside, or under the direction of, national Christians—a commendable balance which, ideally, should demonstrate the unity of the body of Christ.

Taking a world-view, it could justifiably be suggested that Britain and North America are now among the neediest areas of mission. Their culture is post-christian, and secular thought has largely embraced a relativistic outlook, with its consequent abandonment of the absolutes. Taking 'what I like is right' as the norm for living, moral standards plummet and anything goes. In this context, on the one hand divergent sects find a happy hunting ground and on the other syncretistic groupings suggest that we should all get together—although they are not quite sure where we are going, it must, inevitably be the same place. The apostle Paul could never have faced a greater challenge or opportunity.

While missionary strategy would invariably look for areas of potential receptiveness and response to mission, God's sphere of operation is the whole world. It includes the communist blocs, the Muslim world and the ever-expanding Buddhist faith. All three great movements are committed to world mission. Hinduism, while not an evangelistic faith, dominates hundreds of millions of lives. All have one thing in common: they are not waiting to be enlightened and liberated by Christian missionaries. Missionary meetings once lustily sang:

> From Greenland's icy mountains,
> From India's coral strand;

> Where Africa's sunny fountains
> Roll down their golden sand,
> From many an ancient river,
> From many a palmy plain,
> They call us to deliver
> Their land from error's chain.

While the words may promote zeal, they propagate a lie, and have been responsible for bitter disillusionment at the moment of confrontation with Satanic forces.

Some years ago a senior Christian missionary in Pakistan who had seen his only son shot by Muslims whom he had tried to lead to Christ terminated his lecture on Islam with these words: 'If I had served Christ in Pakistan as I ought to have served Him, I would not be alive to give this lecture today.' The book of Acts is not out of date. The experiences of Stephen (ch. 7) and James (ch. 12) belong to this century. What Paul endured in persecution (chs. 14, 16, etc.; cf. II Cor. 11:23–28) and intellectual opposition (ch. 17) is constantly paralleled with terrible consistency.

The question, 'Where is mission?' is not easy to answer in precise terms, for as Paul was called to a specific task (Acts 9:15, 16), so, unerringly, God indicates to individuals His specific will. For most, then, the world of mission will be home, presenting Christ within the context of their own culture; for others it will entail transference to new social and cultural groupings, some enjoying the thrill of ready response to the good news, some knowing hatred, bitterness, death. Christ gave His disciples no reason to expect anything else (cf. John 15:18–20).

Equipment for mission

If the pith helmet has found its way into the dustbin, what has taken its place? Certain basic qualities have always been essential to effective world mission. Without them all the efficiency of the modern missionary machine is worthless.

Devotion, love, a deep concern for others was a prime

requirement of God for Israel. 'Love the sojourner' stipulated Deuteronomy 10:19. The person outside the nation of Israel would recognise God's love only when he saw it in God's people. A missionary running a publishing house in Pakistan seemed to have everything buttoned up; every hour was packed with activity, organizing a literature programme and expounding Scripture. It seemed great until an honest Pakistani commented, 'You can do things more efficiently than we can, but somehow I feel that you don't really love us.' He was right. Jesus Christ was not coming across; just an efficient missionary image.

Failure in mission frequently stems, not so much from a lack of love; love is there but the direction is faulty. The Skid Row incident repeats itself around the world where the evangelical Christian loves the Muslim, the Hindu, the Sikh simply as a 'soul' for whom Christ died and fails to love him as a whole person. It takes no time at all for the Muslim to discover if one is after (in his eyes) another 'convert', or whether there exists a deep concern for the conditions in which he lives, his family problems, his interests, hopes and fears, as well as his spiritual destiny. Together with the preaching and teaching of John the Baptist, Jesus Christ, the apostles and those who worked with them, was an evident concern for people as *persons* (Luke 3:10–13; Matt. 5; John 8:1–11; I Cor. 9:19–23; Gal. 6:10).

The man or woman who comes to Christ in an alien culture needs to be integrated into the Christian community in the entirety of his personality, a community which will care deeply about his social security and needs. He is not only 'in Christ', he is in the 'body of Christ', and the mutual responsibilities within the body demonstrated in I Corinthians 12, and culminating in the demanding requirements of verses 25, 26, have fundamental social implications. How deeply this was felt by the apostle Paul is seen in the amount of space he devotes in his Corinthian correspondence to fund-raising for the destitute Jerusalem Christians (I Cor. 16; II Cor. 9) and his deep concern over the sufferings and needs of others (II Cor. 11:28, 29). World mission demands total involvement with those to whom one is sent. Such involvement tests love, and the other eight fruits of the Spirit (Gal. 5:22, 23), to the limit.

Evangelism in crowded bazaars, handing out literature, or preaching in less crowded churches may make contacts, stimulate interest, promote growth. On the other hand, it may offend—sometimes unnecessarily—closing minds that might otherwise have responded to the good news about Jesus Christ. World mission demands not only the indispensable fruit of the Spirit, it calls for the hard grind of study that opens the mind to an appreciative understanding of the cultural and religious background of those among whom one works.

In the Christian section of a Pakistani village a hundred or so Muslims kindly came to listen to the news of Jesus Christ. Faced with the glorious challenge of such an opportunity the young missionary commenced, 'I believe that Jesus Christ is the Son of God'. These were true words, maybe brave words, but certainly foolish words, for to any Muslim it was blasphemy, implying that God had had sexual intercourse with a woman. And quite apart from anything else, they bluntly denied a basic tenet of Islam, that Allah neither begets nor is begotten. The missionary escaped with his life, but a hundred Muslims' ears were closed to what might have been a life-giving proclamation, because someone had failed to communicate truth in terms which could be understood correctly by those who listened.

Similarly, what use is it in an initial contact to quote the wonderful words of John 3:16 promising eternal life, to a Hindu, whose one desire is to break the cycle of reincarnations and achieve oblivion?

There is a way into the mind, heart and life of men and women of all cultures and creeds; Christ's message is relevant to all humanity. Once understood, that message may still be rejected; but the responsibility to communicate it intelligently rests squarely on the shoulders of the Christian communicator.

It is not sufficient to write off the Muslim or the Hindu with the excuse that he is hard to reach. This failure to communicate meaningfully strikes home with solemn force when one is reminded that Britain lies within the sphere of world mission. Here is a country characterized by middle-class Christianity, where evangelistic techniques and local church structures are most meaningful to the middle-class community, but leave the vast mass of the working-classes virtually untouched, This situation has prompted John Benington in *Culture, Class and Christian Beliefs* to suggest that facing such a situation many Christians are tempted to put the ball into Calvin's court, 'and to retire gracefully with a renewed sense of the mystery of God's sovereign purposes in "election"! But to explain the apparent failure of the Christian gospel to become real to working-class young people "would be to assume a remarkable predilection on God's part for the middle-classes, and a singular distaste for, let us say, industrial workers".'[1]

The problem of making the Christian faith understandable and relevant in working-class Britain, the Muslim world and Hindu India is complex and there are no easy answers; but one cannot write these off as areas of divine indifference. However difficult the task may be, important prerequisites for getting to grips with such situations are an immersion in and identification with the social, religious, cultural and ethnic groupings with which one is seeking to communicate. Jesus Christ pointed the way: 'He himself knew what was in man' (John 2:25), and, 'the great throng heard him gladly' (Mark 12:37). Paul succeeded in getting on to the wavelength of cultures other than his own, immersed as he was in the world of his day. Acts 17:16–34 deserves careful study in this connection. While some have viewed this as one of Paul's less successful experiences, few Christian communicators would grumble if, on entering a new area, they were to see results similar to those of verse 34.

So brief a treatment of the church and world mission inevitably leaves much unsaid, and can only be viewed as an introductory paper.[2] Such important subjects as the role of Christians and churches in political involvement and social action remain untouched. These are areas of life, among many others, which call for active participation as the church lives in the world at home or overseas.

NOTES

1 Here he quotes E. R. Wickham, *Church and People in an Industrial City*
2 See Bibliography for Further Reading

10

Christian Unity

F. R. COAD

The doctrine of Christian unity is not an abstract ideal, remote from the workaday levels of ordinary life: it is an intensely practical doctrine, postulating a basic understanding of human life and human purpose that directly affects our behaviour and our attitudes to our fellow men. A misunderstanding of 'election' has at times obscured this basic assumption, which is that redemption is the consummation of God's plan for mankind, the restoration of His ideal for all men that man's fall frustrated.

If we believe that redeemed mankind is united in one body, of which its Redeemer is head, we imply therefore that the Creator intended and shaped all men with the potential for that unity. So it is that we read in I Timothy 2:4 that God 'desires all men to be saved and to come to the knowledge of the truth'; and so Paul writes in Romans 5:15 that as 'many' died through one man's trespass, so the free gift of grace has abounded for the same 'many'; or, even more daringly in I Corinthians 15:22 that 'as in Adam all die, so also in Christ shall all be made alive'.

If this is God's purpose and design, then men have not been created as solitary creatures, living their lives in individualistic isolation of soul, destined to the despair of ultimate loneliness; rather, they have been created for God and for each other.

Unity and Individuality
That each man is a unique individual is a fact, not only of experience, but of both biology and theology. But the assumption concerning man's nature that underlies the doctrine of

113

the unity of the redeemed implies that man is much more than an individual. It insists that men, all men, are creatures intended and shaped for a unity that transcends their individuality. If this is true, and if men do not attain the true unity for which they were made, then we may expect that they will seek and find a unity of sorts in substitute ways; and such, experience proves.

It is significant that Paul carefully guards this dual aspect of man's being. 'We, though many, are one body in Christ, and *individually* members one of another' (Rom. 12:5). Again, 'Now you are the body of Christ and *individually* members of it' (I Cor. 12:27). Karl Barth comments on the first of these two passages that 'Paul does not set forth individual human personalities as "partial" things comprehended in a larger whole, as so many cells are united into one living organism', but rather that 'the *believers*—men in relation to God—are therefore, in their full grown and in no way attenuated individuality, ONE BODY, ONE INDIVIDUAL in Christ. They are not a mass of individuals, not even a corporation, a personified society, or a "totality", but The Individual, The One, The New Man (I Cor. 12:12, 13).'[1] These two concepts, of unviolated individuality and of unfragmented unity, give us an important clue to the mode in which Christian unity is likely to express itself. What is true of the individual man and the One Body, is also true (if in a modified sense) of the individual congregation and of the One Body. As Alford comments on I Corinthians 12:27, '*Each church* is said to be *the body of Christ*, as each is said to be *the temple of God . . .* ; not that there are many bodies or many temples; but that each church is an image of the whole aggregate, a microcosm, having the same characteristics.'[2]

This dual insight into man's individuality and designed unity is vital to Christianity, as it is vital to the health of the society in which we live. It denies to the Christian and to the church the extremes both of a totalitarianism which would submerge and suppress the individual, and of an individualism that might adopt the cry of Cain—'Am I my brother's keeper?' It is no accident that the New Testament's one recorded evangelistic address to a wholly pagan audience starts with this same fundamental conception of wider human unity: 'He made from one every nation of men to live on all the face of the earth' (Acts 17:26). So it is that Christianity, rightly understood, on the one hand must forbid suppression of the rights of the individual or dissenter, and on the other hand must forbid indulgence in racism or a narrow nationalism, and must commit its adherents to the pursuit of equity and justice in society. The unity of the redeemed cannot and must not be understood as a separatist and elitist doctrine. Although the church must struggle with the gates of Hades to the end of its earthly path, it must never war with its fellow men, for that unity which it cherishes it holds in trust for all mankind, and it must welcome to that unity every one who calls Jesus 'Lord'.

An Essential Biblical Truth

The unity of all Christians in the one Body of Christ is an essential and basic feature of biblical doctrine. If it should be objected that the passages already quoted from Romans and Corinthians have the local congregation in view, we can supplement them from the wide horizons of Ephesians 4:4 ff.: 'There is one body and one Spirit, just as you were called to the one hope that belongs to your call, one Lord, one faith, one baptism, one God and Father of us all. . . .' Yet it is idle to quote proof-texts, when the truth is woven into the very fabric of biblical teaching. Scripture contemplates only one church, and it is scarcely too much to say that the Biblical doctrine of the church collapses without this truth. 'Is Christ divided?' Paul asked of the quarrelling Corinthians (I Cor. 1:13), and the question permits only one answer.

To state these facts in the face of the apparently divided state of Christianity today is to raise a question which must be the burden of any contemporary study of Christian unity. The visible church of Christ seems hopelessly divided: presenting different faces to the world in forms of worship, in doctrine, in church organisation and government, and in testimony to the world. Given the strong emphasis in the

E

New Testament on the divine action in the unity of the church (by one Spirit we were all baptized into one body' I Cor. 12:13) we are forced to ask ourselves whether God's work has failed. Or, if we seek for an alternative to that conclusion, we are driven to ask other questions. Are all, or some, of the apparent differences in fact a sign of disunity, or are we confusing unity and uniformity? If only some, which are the differences which are a breach of unity? Are there differences which go to the root of church-hood, so that those on the wrong side of the divide are Christians—or at least church members—no longer? This leads to another question: is the Church co-terminous with the bounds of Christian profession, or are there Christians outside the church? If the last question is valid, then does the doctrine of unity extend to the church, or to the whole body of Christians? What is unity, and how is it expressed?

To ask these questions is to bring us to the questions to which this study will seek a Biblical answer. What is the basis of unity? Who are those who are united? What is the nature of the unity they constitute? How is this unity realized and expressed in outward practice? A short study can only rehearse the Biblical evidence, and try to summarize the pointers it provides to the answers.

Identification with Christ
The letter to the Galatians comes to us red-hot from the crucible of a new understanding of the ways of God with men. The theory that regards it as the earliest of the extant writings of the apostle Paul is perhaps reinforced when we find that it contains the embryo of a doctrine of the Body of Christ that develops throughout the Pauline writings.. The embryonic doctrine can be traced at the end of the autobiographical section of the letter (2:11–21). Verses 15 and 16 contain Paul's personal testimony to his own experience of justification; but it is important to notice that he appeals to his experience as one common to Peter, to Paul himself and to their audience (if the verses form part of his public conversation with Peter) or to himself and his readers (if it

forms part of his comment on that incident). 'We ourselves...
have believed in Christ Jesus, in order to be justified by
faith in Christ, and not by works of the law.' As the passage
develops from this declaration, he unfolds his deeper understanding of the results of this personal commitment to Christ:
'I through the law died to the law, that I might live to God.
I have been crucified with Christ; it is no longer I who live,
but Christ who lives in me; and the life I now live in the
flesh I live by faith in the Son of God, who loved me and
gave Himself for me.'

So Paul expresses his sense of personal identification with
Christ; an identification so powerful that it involves him, as it
were, in the physical dying of Christ: 'I through the law died
. . . I have been crucified with Christ.' The implicit
identification, almost crude in its vividness, with the crucified
body of Christ, is later (as we shall see) made explicit in the
Roman letter (and see Gal. 5:24 and 6:14). Yet it is an
identification also with the risen life of Christ: 'It is no longer
I who live, but Christ who lives in me.'

The implications of this personal testimony become plain as
the argument of the letter proceeds. In the next chapter the
experience which Paul has postulated of himself personally is
extended to every believer. Christ, in suffering the curse of
the 'hanging on the tree', · has redeemed 'us'—Jew and
Gentile alike (Gal. 3:13, 14). Taking up the symbol of
baptism (which in Romans 6 is explained as the enacted
figure of identification with the death, burial and resurrection
of Christ), he writes, 'As many of you as were baptized into
Christ have put on Christ.' Here again, it is a vivid
identification, a 'clothing oneself' with Christ. But, because
this identification with Christ is shared by every believer, it
becomes the making-one-in-Christ of every believer; 'There is
neither Jew nor Greek, there is neither slave nor free, there is
neither male nor female; for you are all one in Christ Jesus'
(Gal. 3:27, 28).

One Loaf, One Body
Moving on to the first letter to the Corinthians, which may

well be the next of the relevant letters in chronological order also, we find the second great Christian symbol taken as the expression of the same unity; and again that unity is achieved by common identification with the crucified Christ. 'The cup of blessing which we bless, is it not a participation in the blood of Christ? The bread which we break, is it not a participation in the body of Christ? Because there is one bread, we who are many are one body, for we all partake of the one bread' (I Cor. 10:16, 17). Baptism, as an act, was individual: this is communal, a sharing in the one loaf; and so the eucharistic loaf, which is the body of Christ, becomes the community of believers (in some renderings explicitly so, see KJV and RV). This identity of body and community becomes the ground of practical exhortation in chapter 12, where the metaphor of the body is used to emphasize the lessons of mutual interdependence of gift within the local church, leading to the verse we have already quoted 'you are the body of Christ, and individually members of it' (I Cor. 12:27).

There is a further significant development in 1 Corinthians 12. Again, the symbol of baptism appears, but now the Spirit is seen as the uniting power of the body, indeed, as the author of that unity and perhaps even as the very element in which the baptizing takes place. 'By one Spirit we were all baptized into one body—Jews or Greeks, slaves or free—and all were made to drink of one Spirit (1 Cor. 12:13). So the declaration of Galatians 3:27, 28 is extended and transmuted: and what was implicit there ('put on Christ . . . you are all one') is made explicit here ('into one body'). The risen life of Christ of Galatians 2:20 is seen as the very life of the Spirit of God. We have not only a shared experience of justification and a shared participation in Christ, but a shared and experienced new dimension of life itself (1 Cor. 12:4–11).

In the letter to the Romans, which probably followed not long after the first Corinthian letter, there are further developments. First, the identification with the crucified body of Christ, implicit (as we have seen) in Galatians, is made explicit. In Galatians, Paul had declared that he had 'died to the law' and been 'crucified with Christ' (2:19, 20). Now, in Romans 7:4, the two statements are fused, 'Likewise, my brethren, you have died·to the law through the body of Christ.' In Romans 12, he takes up the same image of the body which he had used of the local church in I Corinthians, but with a difference. There, he had had particularly in mind the internal gifts of the church, gifts of public service and leadership within the church: here, the list ranges more widely, progressing to the more personal virtues of giving, showing mercy, brotherly love, the tenor of daily living and mutual hospitality and care—leading on in chapter 13 to the context of the whole world in which the church lives, its total environment of political and social relationships. It is still the local church, yet it is also wider than that. It is the body of Christ in the world, standing in a definite relationship to the world, and inter-acting with it.

Cosmic Dimensions

The way is thus open for the culmination of the doctrine which is contained in the later 'prison epistles' of Paul's closing years. The very restriction of his bodily movement has left the apostle's spirit free to roam the heavenly places. In Ephesians 1 the ages unroll before the mind of the apostle, and at their centre is Christ (v. 10); but there, *in* Christ, is the church—not now the local church, but the church universal, the inheritance of Christ: the church 'which is His body, the fulness of Him who fills all in all' (vv. 11–14, 18–23). This church is the means by which 'the manifold wisdom of God might now be made known to the principalities and powers in the heavenly places' (Eph. 3:10). The church is united to Christ as one flesh, so that husband and wife in their ideal unity are but a picture of what that unity is in reality: 'We are members of His body'—(and, some manuscripts add, 'of His flesh and of His bones') (Eph. 5:28–30).

Yet the original thought of Galatians is still there, underlying the magnificence of the cosmic concept. The reconciliation of Jew and Gentile, the abolition of that archetype

119

of every 'dividing wall of hostility', into 'one new man', into 'one body', is 'through the cross'; and the estranging law is abolished 'in his flesh' (Eph. 2:11–16). We are back, at the consummation, at the same truth from which the embryonic doctrine was born (Gal. 2:19, 20). Here, at the richest development of the truth of Christian unity, there still stands the central fact of the reconciling cross of Christ.

These are profound truths and they open up a pathway into the depths of an understanding of the Incarnation and of its implications for the church and for mankind. But that is not our present pathway. We have concentrated on these Pauline scriptures that develop the truth of the One Body, because they are essential to an understanding of the subject of Christian unity. They illuminate for us the full significance and poignancy of the great foundation declarations by our Lord Himself: the prayer of John 17, and the central passage of Matthew 16:13 ff. I have explored the latter passage more fully elsewhere,[3] and here we need only notice the fact, confirming all that we have discovered hitherto, that the church is, by our Lord's own declaration, the building and creation of Christ Himself. It is worthy of note that this central passage of Matthew is followed immediately by the account of the Transfiguration—an account in which another writer, studying the use of the word 'overshadow' in the New Testament, has seen the 'conception' as it were of the church which was to come to birth at Pentecost (compare Luke 1:35 with Matthew 17:5).[4] The setting of the account of the Transfiguration in the presence of Peter, James and John, the three embryonic figures of the church, and immediately after the declaration of Caesarea Philippi, increases the pertinence of this insight, and adds to the meaning of the Transfiguration a dimension that is of profound and suggestive significance.

Conclusion
This brief survey of Biblical teaching is sufficient to illuminate a pathway to the solution of the questions posed at the start. The basis of unity is a shared personal experience and

confession of Christ; a unity symbolized and consolidated by baptism and the Lord's Supper. Those who are united are all those who share that personal experience and confession of Christ, and they are united by His own act, by His Spirit, in His body. This very definition makes it impossible that any who share that committal to Christ should be excluded from the unity in Him. The unity is a unity of life, and therefore expresses itself in all the variety of life. It is demonstrated in witness and service to the community and to the world. In essence it is not cultic or institutional; though cult and institution may each be means of expressing it, the limitations inherent in every human situation mean that they can never be more than a partial and temporary expression of the fulness of the unity.

No attempt at expressing the unity of the church in institutional forms can be expected to be successful unless it recognizes and respects the sovereignty of the acts of God which constitute unity, and is prepared to subject its ambitions and its methods to those acts of God. Perennially, and in all brands of churchmanship, the mind and thought of man is apt to attempt to over-ride and control the acts of God: but that temptation is as presumptious and as impossible and disastrous as man's attempt to defy the acts of God in nature. But to the humble, who are prepared to respect and understand the realities and ways of God, those very laws of God are given as the tools to accomplish unimagined blessing.

NOTES

1 See the whole of his comment on Romans 12:3–5 in *The Epistle to the Romans* Hoskyns trans. (1933), pp. 441–444

2 *The Greek New Testament* (1856), *in loc.*

3 'The Apostolic Church' *A New Testament Commentary* ed. G. C. D. Howley (1969), pp. 102–103

4 Maisie Spens, in *Receive the Joyfulness of Your Glory*, (1952), as quoted by and commented on by Michael Marshall in 'Confrontation and Transfiguration' in *Christian*, Vol. 1, No. 2 (1973), pp. 107–114

11

The Church and Israel

H. L. ELLISON

The justification for this chapter in a symposium on the church comes from widespread disagreement on the position and role of Israel, or the Jews, in God's plan and purposes for salvation. Broadly speaking, the attitude of the unreformed churches and those that have followed their traditions, including the Lutherans, is that God rejected the Jews and handed over their position and privileges to the church, which is the new Israel, the true Israel, or Israel after the spirit. The Calvinistic tradition asserts that just as the New Covenant is merely the continuation of the Old, so the church is merely the continuation of Israel, for its elect remnant in the first century A.D. simply formed the nucleus of Christ's church, which can therefore be called Israel without qualification. There are others, though they have always formed a minority, who have maintained that the purpose of the two bodies has always been different and so each will continue to accomplish God's purpose in separate roles to the end of time.

A study of these views would demand far too much space. We shall, however, be able to understand the biblical teaching better if we glance at the development of the problem in the first two centuries of the church's life.

An Overview of Early Church History
After the return from the Babylonian exile the Jewish community in Palestine became increasingly divided, especially during and after the persecutions under Antiochus IV Epiphanes (175–163 B.C.). By the time of Christ we can distinguish Sadducees, Pharisees, Essenes or Qumran

122

Covenanters and Zealots, but all these seem to have been further subdivided, and there were smaller groups as well.

For the early church the practical importance of this was that Jewry was divided into a number of mutually hostile groups, each claiming to be the true depository of Israel's traditions, in some cases going so far as to refuse table fellowship to others, yet none claiming to be exclusively Israel. The rise of the first Christians simply added another group to their number. Though they were convinced that they alone had experienced the hope of Israel, they no more claimed to be Israel, to the exclusion of those Jews who did not accept Jesus as Messiah, than did the other groups. They claimed that the religion of the others was incomplete and in part erroneous, but not that it was basically false.

The position was not changed by the spread of the gospel to the Samaritans, who were regarded as schismatic Jews, or to the occasional Gentile like Cornelius, who was already on the fringe of the synagogue. It was in Antioch that the disciples were first called Christians, which means that in some way they were differentiated in the popular mind from the synagogue. The rapid inflow of Gentile converts included many who knew little of Judaism and had no particular love for Jews. They had been attracted not by the superior ethics of the synagogue or by its imageless monotheism, but by the power of the risen Christ to forgive, heal and restore. They knew that they were linked with the hopes of Israel, for they were expected to know the main Messianic passages of the Old Testament, but hardly those linked with Jewry's specific interests.

The solution worked out in Antioch for establishing harmony between Jews and Gentiles in the church and carried by Barnabas and Paul to Cyprus and Asia Minor (Galatia) was soon ratified in Jerusalem (Acts 15). It was recognized that the church was a new Messianic community in which Jews and Gentiles participated on equal terms. The only concession asked of the latter was the observance of the Noachic commandments, that is that they would avoid practices which would make close fellowship with Jewish

123

believers very difficult and would scandalize the local synagogue, making it unwilling to hear the gospel. The church
clearly saw itself in a central position, holding out a hand to
both Jews and Gentiles; this by itself would have inhibited
any tendency to think of itself as Israel.

In the past some have laid great stress on the practical
advantages that came to the church by its association in the
official mind with the synagogue. These were because
Judaism was a *religio licita*, an officially permitted religion,
and because from the time of Julius Caesar Jews enjoyed
certain privileges. The latter may be dismissed out of hand,
for whatever these privileges, they could hardly have been
claimed by anyone not vouched for by the local Jewish
community.

The well-known situation mirrored in Pliny's correspondence with the emperor Trajan (*c.* 110), in which he asked
how he should deal with Christians, is obviously a new one,
which had in fact arisen from a stricter supervision of all
'societies'. In the time of Paul it is improbable that the
authorities were interested in the religion of their subjects,
especially when they were not Roman citizens and as much
on the fringe of society as were the majority of the early
Gentile Christians.

The only incident in the New Testament that can be
appealed to for the *religio licita* idea is the bringing of Paul
before Gallio (Acts 18:12–17). There is no suggestion, however, that the status of the church in Corinth was being
questioned; the synagogue was concerned with Paul's activities, and by both Jewish and Roman law he was a Jew.
The standing of those Christians who were Jews neither by
Roman nor Jewish law was not being called in question. In
the Neronian persecution (64) it was known that the
Christians were not Jews, but they were condemned osten-
sibly as incendiaries and not for their religion.

The main steps in the entire separation between the church
and the synagogue are clear enough. The Jewish War of 66–
70 made it increasingly embarrassing for a Gentile Christian
to be taken as a Jew. The rabbis in Yabneh (Jamnia) *c.* 90

made it virtually impossible for a Jewish Christian to remain a synagogue member and so slowed down the intake of Jewish members into the church. This was aggravated by the slide of a large section of Palestinian Jewish Christians into heresy. The recognition by the Jews of Bar Kochba as Messiah in the revolt of 132–135 was decisive. It finally drove the Jewish Christians from the synagogue and caused the church to regard the Jew as not merely failing to recognize Jesus as Messiah but as positively choosing a false one. On political grounds dissociation from the Jews became even more desirable.

Along with the separation of the church and Israel came the problem created by Marcion (c. 150). He was a bishop's son from Pontus, who in due course arrived in Rome teaching that the only value of the Old Testament was a historical one, and that it had no spiritual purpose for the Christian. The God of the Old Testament was not the God and Father of our Lord Jesus Christ.

Though the church emphatically repudiated Marcion's teaching, it found it difficult to explain why it retained the Old Testament. The easiest way out was not to repudiate the God but the people of the Old Covenant, and to claim that the church was the true Israel. Such language is not found before 150, but it soon became generally accepted and has continued down to our time.

New Testament Teaching
The terms Israel, Israelite are used relatively little in the New Testament, 77 times in all. The ethnic term Jew is used when Jew and Gentile meet, and so it is the usual term in writings which were intended in the main for non-Jewish readers. When Jews speak together, we find Israel (cf. Matt. 27:42; John 1:49; 12:13 with Matt. 2:2; 27:11, 29, 37; John 18:33). It is used also when the concept of the people of God is being stressed. The most obvious example of this is the use of Israel, with three exceptions where the ethnic stress is uppermost, in Romans 9–11, in contrast to the use of Jew in the earlier chapters.

The church is founded on Christ's death and resurrection, hence we have little more than allusions to its nature in the gospels. For our purpose the most important is, 'I have other sheep, that are not of this fold; I must bring them also, and they will heed My voice. So there shall be one flock, one shepherd' (John 10:16). The alternation of fold and flock is a clear indication that Christ can have His people in more than one group. (Note that the AV rendering, 'one fold, one shepherd', is based not on any Greek MSS, but on an early Latin distortion; it both misses the meaning and has been the excuse for much persecution).

The widening of the church, first to the Samaritans, then to 'God-fearers' on the fringe of the synagogue, and finally to the heathen world in all its darkness, idolatry and abominations, was God's act and was accepted as such. The Jews had all along expected some form of conversion of the Gentiles in the Messianic age, and Jesus was the Messiah. But the Old Testament had never suggested that the nations that would flow to Jerusalem would become Jews. Israel remained Israel and paramount (cf. Isa. 19:24, 25).

Paul's offence to Jews who rejected Jesus and to many who accepted Him was twofold. It was not that he did not seek to impose the Law on Gentiles. It was that he put a Gentile who believed in Jesus on the same level as the Law-observant Jew who did; and, worse still, that he put him above a Law-observant Jew who rejected Him. There is not the least ground for the accusation against Paul, believed by so many in the Jerusalem church (Acts 21:20, 21); yet the very fact that it was believed shows that it expressed the inescapable logic of completely subordinating the Law to the Messiah. The usual rabbinic view was that Messiah's chief task, apart from freeing Israel, was the enforcing of the Law.

Had it been possible to postulate two peoples of God, two churches, two flocks, the problem would have created little difficulty. But for Israel to be only a fold within the one flock demanded a complete rethinking of its position. Already John the Baptist had prophetically pointed to the solution: 'God is able from these stones to raise up children to Abraham'

(Luke 3:8), where the stones were, above all, the stony-hearted Gentiles.

Abraham was not a Jew, not an Israelite, not under the Law, though the rabbis fabled that he knew and kept the Law, even though it had not been given. Abraham was the first to give a full example of faith reckoned as righteousness. Jesus, the promised seed, had given the foundation for that faith which leads to righteousness, and so the Messianic people of God all stand on the same footing and are Abraham's offspring (Gal. 3:6–29; Rom. 4:1–17).

The apparently obvious deduction made by many was that the Jew had served his purpose and therefore had no more meaningful existence. But this accords neither with New Testament teaching nor Jewish history. Paul insisted that 'the gifts and the call of God are irrevocable' (Rom. 11:29). Of the gifts he summarized (Rom. 3:2; 9:4, 5) most were not given to Abraham, and Paul was clear that they were Israel's continuing possession, even though the church shares in most of them. The only one we could reasonably claim has been annulled in practice is the (Temple) worship. At least for the present (see below) the church stands higher than Israel. Therefore, the honorific titles of Israel belong to the church also (cf. I Pet. 2:9 with Exod. 19:5, 6), but that does not mean that they have first to be taken from Israel. Jesus is the fulfilment of all that Israel stands for; hence He can cause the church to enjoy all that was promised to Israel without depriving Israel of it.

Paul, however, stresses that when he writes of Israel he does not mean Jews without qualification. Throughout Scripture the idea that God can in any way be bound or even influenced by the purely physical is opposed. Yet to this day we meet the idea among Christians that the mere fact of Jewish parentage carries with it the necessity of God's favour or curse, according to the individual's theological prejudices.

For Paul it is self-evident that 'not all who are descended from Israel (that is Jacob) belong to Israel' (Rom. 9:6). Just as only Isaac of the children of Abraham, and Jacob and not Esau carried forward God's redemptive purpose, so mere physical descent from Jacob could not possibly guarantee that any individual Israelite would be a true member of Israel, the people of God. This is implicitly recognized by the Jews, for at all times the proselyte has been given equal status with the Jewish born, thus indicating that birth was not the decisive factor.

We normally find the Old Testament election of a people contrasted with the New Testament election of individuals, but this is an over-simplification. In the New Testament, individuals are elected to be formed into the church, the people of God. In the Old, we have the elect nation to begin with, but both in history and prophecy the message is that within this nation there is a continuous election being carried out. It narrows down to Jesus Christ only to expand again to embrace the church in the New. Both visible Israel and the visible church are larger than the true election within them, and in neither case can the beholder be sure where the line of separation is to be drawn.

Not merely are Israel and the church linked in a common process of election, but they are interlinked parts in a complex plan of salvation. For Israel's experience of national salvation in the Exodus, Pharaoh's heart had to be hardened (Rom. 9:17, 18). In due course it was Israel's turn for it to be hardened in part (Rom. 11:7, 25; AV 'blinded' misses the parallelism), so that salvation might come to the Gentiles and the world be reconciled to God (Rom. 11:11, 15). When God's purpose in their hardening had been accomplished,[1] then 'all Israel will be saved'.

We must notice that this hardening is affirmed not merely of Jewry in general but also of the true people of God within it, the people of God's election, part of which passes into the church, but the other part continues in its hardening within Jewry. Then this hardening is more than once linked with the vision of Isaiah at his call (Isa. 6:9, 10; Matt. 13:14, 15; Mark 4:12; John 12:37–41; Acts 28:25–27). Of these passages the most important is that in John, for it makes explicit that the hardening was not the punishment for the rejection of Christ but the cause of it.

With a strange perverseness most translations of Romans 11:15 render 'their rejection', or an equivalent so far as meaning is concerned, so making Paul contradict his clear statement in Romans 11:1, where he flatly denies any such rejection (in Greek different words are used). The meaning would be best expressed by 'their being put to one side'. Once we grasp that there is no question of rejection or repudiation, but simply on non-use, then we should find no difficulty in the statement that at the coming of Christ 'all Israel shall be saved'. This is not an affirmation that all Jews will be saved, for salvation can never be bound up with a race and human descent; but that all God's elect people within Jewry, not merely those at Christ's coming, but also throughout their history, will be saved. God's purpose in election will be completely vindicated, and it will be a bold person who will affirm that this salvation will differ in any essential from that of the church, especially if we take Romans 11:31 into consideration.

The usual Christian interpretation of Romans 11:26 is that Paul foresees the final swallowing up of the remnants of Israel in the glorified church. If that is what Paul meant, he could have expressed it more clearly. But in Romans 11:12, 15 he has clearly implied that the coming to faith of Israel has a special part to play in the future blessing and welfare of the world, and there is no valid reason for doubting that Paul considered that Israel, not the church, would yet accomplish the glowing promises of blessing in the prophets, that is that saved Israel had yet a purpose to fulfil.

The opponents of the idea that this earth has a future after the coming of Christ base themselves either on the depreciation of the material derived from Greek thought, or on the relatively rare mention of it in the New Testament. The latter can be explained easily enough by its being primarily a concern of saved Israel rather than of the glorified church. This is not the place to discuss why it should be Israel's task rather than the church's beyond saying that the world has yet to see a redeemed people, in contrast to redeemed individuals, living out the perfect will of God perfectly.

129

The maintenance of Israel as a special entity even at the coming of Christ must, however, not be thought of as something permanent. The final chapters of the Bible show us heaven and earth linked by 'the holy city, new Jerusalem', which has come down from heaven, 'the Bride, the wife of the Lamb' (Rev. 21:9), that is the glorified church. In its symbolic description we find that though its twelve foundations bear the names of the twelve apostles of the Lamb, its twelve gates carry the names of the twelve tribes of the sons of Israel. In other words, in eternity the church and Israel have amalgamated.

Mankind always oversimplifies the problems that face him. He may seek a solution in an unresolvable dualism, a sort of 'East is East and West is West, and never the twain shall meet' attitude; or he seeks to eliminate the obstacles—the lion lies down with the lamb—inside him! The Christian should realize that all these problems find their final solution in Jesus Christ, in whom the perfect wisdom of God is displayed (Rom. 11:33–36). In Him too the apparent barrier between Jew and Gentile, between church and synagogue, between Old and New, between preparation and fulfilment find their solution.

Additional Note

Popular exegesis affirms that Paul actually calls Christians 'the Israel of God' in Galatians 6:16. So much is this the case that it is expressly affirmed by slipshod translation in RSV, Phillips, Jer. B., TEV. We should always beware of basing any theory on a unique phrase, and so there have always been scholars who have taken the Israel of God to refer to Jewish Christians. It is, however, difficult to see why they should be specially referred to here and only here by this term.

Very few have taken seriously that exceptionally Paul places peace before mercy, which is theologically the wrong order. Both difficulties are met by following Richardson[2] and translating, 'As many as shall walk by this rule, peace be upon them, and mercy upon the Israel of God.' In this case 'the Israel of God' is simply the election Israel of Romans 9–11 which has not yet come to faith in Christ.

NOTES

1 For a discussion of 'the fulness of the Gentiles' (Rom. 11:25) see my *Mystery of Israel* (1968) pp. 90–92

2 Peter Richardson, *Israel in the Apostolic Church* (1969), a highly scholarly study of the use of Israel in the New Testament and early Christian writers

12

The Church and the World

Christianity has been well described as the most materialistic of the world's religions. Perhaps the most obvious support for this conclusion is found in the doctrine of the Incarnation, which affirms that the eternal Word of God became flesh. But behind this distinctively New Testament belief lies the Old Testament attitude to the created world, which is grounded in the early chapters of Genesis. During the last century these have too often been regarded merely as a battlefield in the supposed warfare between science and religion with the result that their religious teaching has often been overlooked. Yet in fact they are the foundation for all biblical (and thus for all truly Christian) thinking about the world.

Genesis 1–3

First of all, Genesis 1–3 affirms that the material world is not an illusion. It really exists in objective reality. It is separate from God although upheld and sustained by His power (Col. 1:17). He made it and it expresses His will, power, wisdom and love.

Second, Genesis 1–3 asserts that the world is good. Five times in Genesis 1:1–25 this is simply stated, and the final 'very good' of verse 31 displays the satisfaction of the artist or craftsman at the final perfection of a job well done. Nowhere in Scripture, we should note, is this basic goodness of the world denied. While it is true that because of sin 'the whole creation groans and travails together' yet still 'the heavens declare the glory of God', the psalmist can see God's wisdom and love all round him (as in for example Psalm 104), and Paul affirms that 'everything created by God is good and to be received with thanksgiving' (I Tim. 4:4f). Nor does the Bible anywhere suggest that the creation is merely of temporary concern to God. Even at the end and goal of time there are to be new heavens and earth—an immeasurable contrast to the more 'spiritual' goals of some non-Christian religions.

Within this material and good world, man has a distinctive place. To start with, he is part of creation. Psalm 148 shows man uniting with snow, angels, trees and stars to praise God. Francis of Assisi was thoroughly biblical when he spoke of Brother Fire and Sister Water. In this sense, man is one with whatever else is in the created world, and science is so far right to treat man as subject to the same 'laws of nature' as everything else in the universe. Like the animals, he is said to have been made from the earth (Gen. 1:24; 2:7). Yet these two passages also set man apart from other living creatures. The distinctive creation word *bara* is used of him in 1:27. Into his nostrils God breathes the breath of life directly (2:7). He is made in God's image (1:26f) and in this way also differs from the rest of creation. He can thus relate personally to God, hearing, obeying, disobeying, addressing, approaching, loving or hating his Creator. Certainly as creature man ranks with rocks, plants and animals. Yet he also stands over against them because of his unique relationship with God.

In the context, the 'image of God' is related to the command that man exercise authority over the creation. Just as an eastern king would set up his image within his dominions as a sign of his authority within them, so God has placed man as His steward on earth. The tragedy of our raped and disfigured planet is that man has acted as a tyrant rather than a steward.

Yet the so-called 'cultural mandate' of 1:28 is still being fulfilled every day, however incompletely or perversely, by men everywhere. Whenever he formulates a 'law of nature', builds a bridge, paints a picture or digs a garden man is exercising his God-given mandate over creation. Such activities are of immense significance, even when carried on by men and women who are in rebellion against God. Christians

133

might see their human responsibilities rather differently if they accepted them in the spirit of Psalm 8, which is in effect a wondering response to Genesis 1:28.

Man has not been thrown into the world to sink or swim on his own. The Genesis story shows him placed within a network of relationships and responsibilities. First, he is to live in covenant with his Creator. Second, he is to act as steward over the rest of creation. Third, he is to work; this privilege and condition of human fulfilment obligates unfallen man and is in no way a penalty of sin (Gen. 2:15). Fourth, man is male and female, the two together constituting mankind (Gen. 1:27). As for monogamous marriage, this is neither a human invention nor a Christian institution but part of God's plan for mankind (Gen. 2:18–25). (This simple fact has, we may note in passing, important implications for elders of a local church when asked to marry two unbelievers.)

But has sin no effect, the reader may be wondering, on the relationship between man and the world? After all, Genesis 1 and 2 refer to a perfect world; surely sin has modified both mankind and the rest of creation? (cf. Romans 8:19–22). It is, of course, very difficult to specify the effects of sin upon nature. Does Genesis 3:17b, 18, for example, refer to a catastrophic change in nature or to life outside Eden? Quite clearly, human relationships have been poisoned and neither marriage nor work is now an unmixed source of happiness and fulfilment.

So far as man is concerned, Scripture is emphatic about his total depravity. In Romans 3:10–18 Paul collects Old Testament passages bearing on this and later concludes that 'nothing good dwells in me, that is, in my flesh' (Rom. 7:18). Yet although men are 'darkened in their understanding' (Eph. 4:18) and even 'dead through trespasses and sins' (Eph. 2:1), it is never hinted that they no longer show God's image. We may, if we choose, express a truth of Scripture by saying that the image is now distorted and disfigured. Yet, although every aspect of human life is tainted, the Lord Himself assumes that unregenerate man can in some sense do good (Luke 6:33; 11:13; cf. Rom. 2:14f). This does not mean that man is no longer guilty before God and at enmity with Him. But experience and Scripture agree that truth, beauty and goodness may appeal to, and in measure be practised by, men and women who show the divine likeness even though they remain unrepentant. In this connection we may see especial significance in Genesis 4:19–22. These verses ascribe the invention of the arts and technology (specifically of music and metallurgy) to the ungodly line of Cain. We might assume that this implies an adverse judgment on such activities. But in view of their extensive use for worship (see for example Exod. 35:30–36:1) it seems wiser to conclude that we have here an outstanding example of the way in which God shows His love and goodness even to unrepentant sinners (Matt. 5:44f).

Common Grace

Christians have often assumed that God is concerned only about the redemption of the world. But in such passages as those we have mentioned, and in many more, the Bible plainly teaches that He is also active in preserving and renewing the world. Indeed, when we are appalled at the lawlessness apparent both in international relationships and in the social life of many nations we may well thank God for every sign of His common grace working against such influences. This grace may not bring men to new birth, but it displays God's love in preserving some good amidst the corruption of sin.

This distinction between God's common grace which is experienced (though not acknowledged) by all, and his saving grace, is important in several respects. First of all, it goes some way towards solving the problem presented to believers by the apparently admirable spouse, parent or colleague whose goodness is undeniable but who is emphatically not a Christian. In such cases we are tempted to adopt one of two courses: either we try to label the individual as (unconsciously!) Christian or else we cast doubt upon the value of his achievement. It is however more reasonable as well as more biblical to recognize in such behaviour what Francis

135

Schaeffer calls the 'mannishness' of man, which continues to function in spite of sin.

It thus becomes clear also that God is concerned about the whole of human life, not just the 'spiritual' part of it. God made mankind to live within the created order, and to do this is meaningful and satisfying. Scientific research thus means (in Kepler's words) 'thinking God's thought after Him'. Applied science represents one way of fulfilling the command to 'have dominion'.

The Christian's daily work will be undertaken not merely in order to live nor to finance evangelism ('My business is preaching the gospel; I sell insurance to cover expenses'). In the light of Scripture work fulfils God's purpose for man; it is very likely a way of exercising dominion; it should involve serving others in mutual dependence.

Human creativity is another sphere which Christians have sometimes found difficult to locate in their world view. Too often they have professed to regard all except religious art as irrelevant to God's purpose for man or even as sinful. (Yet they have chosen crockery because they liked its shape or colour and have enjoyed a well-planned garden.) Alternatively, their keen sense of beauty has led some to claim that this or that creative genius 'must have' been a Christian 'really'. The Bible teaches us to relate man's creativity and love of beauty to God the Creator. Just as men everywhere have a moral sense because they are made by a God who is righteous, so artistic gifts are experienced and valued all the world over by men who may not even dream that God is the supreme Artist. Here, as in other areas, a man who is rebelling against God may nevertheless do work which is worthwhile and even outstanding. As for their own creativity, Christians will value this the more as they recognize its divine origin.

Social and Political Involvement

Also affected by this distinction between common and saving grace is our understanding of the church's role. Her distinctive work is to proclaim Christ as Saviour by word and action. Her distinctive way of changing human life is through the transforming power of the Holy Spirit. The Bible nowhere suggests that 'kingdom of God' conditions are going to be achieved on earth by human activity except through the Man whose presence or *parousia* will mark the final coming of the Kingdom. Meanwhile, His followers witness to the existence of a kingship which operates quite differently from earthly rule (John 18:36; Mark 9:42–44) and a campaign for which human weapons and tactics are quite inadequate (Eph. 6:11f). The socially transforming power of the gospel can be seen in sixteenth and seventeenth century England and Scotland following the Reformation; the Methodist revival changed much of English life; later revivals have proved how the gospel can work a revolution in a community. By contrast, churches corporately involved in political activity, whether right or left, tend to have little time left for a message of radical inward renewal and may become both spiritually sterile and politically suspect. The records of Greek Orthodoxy, Roman Catholicism, Anglicanism and Lutheranism are in this respect a serious warning.

Part of the difficulty, we may note in passing, is that whenever local churches are linked by some superstructure the new 'church' is expected to pronounce on social issues and tends to lose credibility if it does not. It may also become institutionally involved in economic affairs through massive investments which will apparently need to be safeguarded by practical measures.

This is not to imply that individual Christians should not participate in political activity. Today the state has greater influence than ever before upon the happiness and wellbeing of its citizens, and love for his neighbour must lead the believer to argue and protest as well as pray about injustice and evil in community life. Of course the mere fact that he is a Christian will give him no special competence to suggest what policies will best effect the purposes he approves of. For example, he may protest against policies that cause unemployment both on humane grounds and in the light of Genesis 2:15. Devising measures to remedy this demands a

knowledge of economics in just the same way as bridge
building or medicine are the responsibility of trained specialists. But this is no argument for sitting on the fence and
declining to commit oneself to support specific policies. As we
shall see later, giving Caesar his due in a democratic society
will include prayerfully working for the policies which seem
most likely to build community. Declining to do this may
indicate cowardice or laziness as much as spirituality. After
all, if God is concerned about preserving society then so
should his people be.

A democratic society today is very different from the
totalitarian state of New Testament times. Yet the Bible still
offers guidance to Christians who want to know their duty to
the state and the New Testament attitude is consistent
although superficially ambiguous. Basic is the Saviour's distinction between what is owed to God and what is due to
Caesar (Mark 12:13–17). The coin here represents the benefits of stable government—Caesar's coinage in circulation
shows that his authority is accepted in Judaea; it thus
guarantees economic as well as judicial order. Such benefits
obligate his subjects to have a duty of obedience.

Paul argues in much the same way in Romans 13:1–7,
where he affirms the good done by the state in securing justice
(vv. 1–5) and concludes that conscience obligates the believer
to obey. Paul adds two Old Testament insights. First, he uses
a word, 'powers', which hints here and in I Corinthians 2:8
at the idea that spiritual forces lie behind governments (cf.
Dan. 10:13, 20). Second, he stresses that such authority has
been instituted by God (Rom. 13:1). So, in the normal
course, to disobey lawful authority is to disobey God.

But Jesus also spoke about giving God His due. In view of
the reference to the coin as stamped with Caesar's image it
seems clear that Jesus is saying in effect: 'You are men,
bearing God's image, and to Him you owe your very selves.'
Clearly there are limits to the obedience due to Caesar. And
where we find the New Testament inculcating an attitude to
Rome very different from that of Romans 13, it is because the
command to worship the Emperor has brought about a

situation in which loyalty to God entails disobedience to Caesar. The principle is simply stated in Acts 5:29, and the associated view of a 'power' which is in this respect demonic finds expression in Revelation 13:1–10.

What are the situations in which Christians have felt obliged to disobey the state? The question has arisen very rarely. Paul's words are emphatic and Christians have rightly judged that almost any stable government is better than none. Their responsibility to obey extends beyond matters of morality (for example laws against theft) to fiscal demands (customs duty, income tax) and mere administrative regulations.

Sometimes, however, governments have for various reasons prohibited or unduly limited worship, the circulation of the Scriptures or evangelism. They may even have kept clear of such interference but have committed themselves to policies which were flagrantly evil (for example the Nazi attempt to destroy Jews). Sooner or later the sticking point has come. Christians have not always been able to agree about the precise point when this happened. Some who are pacifists have felt able only to engage in passive resistance, while others have concluded that if a just war against another power is possible, then it may be right to engage in civil war. Dietrich Bonhoeffer, for example, felt compelled to share in the generals' plot against Hitler, although he believed it to be wrong, since non-participation seemed an even greater sin.

It is hard to see why some Christians apparently disapprove of the sort of public demonstration which draws attention to some social evil without breaking any law. Jesus himself was involved in one (Mark 11:15–17). Each case must be judged on its merits.

Besides obeying the authorities Christians are to pray for them. Against a background of persecution Tertullian protested in about AD 200: 'You call us disloyal because we will not swear by Caesar's genius. On the contrary, we rank Caesar above these dead gods of yours and pray for him ... to the God who made him ruler and is alone above him.' The liturgies of the various denominations provide for this, and where extempore prayer is used prayers are offered for the queen and other heads of state and for matters of national concern. Yet most prayer meetings show that by and large believers do not attach much importance to intercession on such topics. A token reference may be made or prayer spasmodically offered for the victims of some recent disaster but no more. This failure may be due to lack of faith or to ignorance of the part played in the nation's life by such bodies as the Trades Union Congress and Confederation of British Industry or the responsibilities of police, Members of Parliament and those who work in the media.

One of the greatest differences between the state in New Testament times and today is the increased opportunity (in some nations) for participation in government. Democracy is biblical, as C. S. Lewis pointed out long ago, because human sin makes it too dangerous to trust any individual or group with unlimited power. And democracy depends on participation. Given a biblical view of the importance of government, it seems clear that among the things 'due' according to Romans 13:7 we must include the intelligent and prayerful use of a democratic citizen's rights. Philippians 3:20 is sometimes quoted against this. The context shows that Paul is warning not against political activity (how could he, in the first century?) but against a materialistic outlook.

It seems as if love to one's neighbour and the obligation to give Caesar his due demand in a democratic society that a man not only work for his living and pay his dues but also take responsibility for using his political rights. This does not mean that God calls every Christian, as he called, for example, Wilberforce and Shaftesbury, to a life of political activity, any more than he calls every Christian to work in any particular role. This means simply that in this sphere also the believer must act as salt.

The World as Evil

Certainly the Christian believer cannot—however much he may wish to do so—escape from the world. Indeed the Lord refused to make this His prayer for His followers (John 17:5). Instead, he asked that they might be kept from the evil. In a similar spirit James exhorts his hearers to be 'unspotted by the world' (1:27). This sombre view of the world, which we have so far largely ignored, is rather common in the New Testament. Paul uses the word *aeon* (age) thus in Romans 12:2, I Corinthians 2:6, 8 and Galatians 1:4. But the thought is characteristic of the Johannine writings, where the normal word *kosmos* is used in this pejorative sense. The world does not know the Saviour (John 1:10) and indeed hates Him and His people (7:4; 15:8f; 17:14) so that to be its friend is to be God's enemy (James 4:4). In fact, all that it contains is evil (I John 2:16). The explanation of this adverse judgment is simple. Satan is the ruler of this world (John 14:30) and it lies in him (I John 5:19). But Jesus has overcome the world (John 16:33) and so shall His followers (I John 5:4). Finally it will pass away (I John 2:17).

Plainly, the word is here being used in a special sense which has to be held simultaneously with the implication of Psalm 104 (although even here, cf. v. 35a) and I Timothy 4:4f. John 3:16 cannot ultimately contradict I John 2:15. In its negative sense, the world is human society based as it is on a rejection of God's loving and righteous authority. The lust of the flesh, the lust of the eye and the pride of life are everywhere to be observed as they have been since Genesis 3:1–6. The ultimate commentary on the whole system is that it crucified Jesus (I Cor. 2:3)—and continues to reject Him. In this sense, Christians are emphatically 'not of the world' (John 17:16). They are obedient to God in a spirit of meekness, whereas the world is proud and rebellious. They see greatness in service; the world in being served. They know the satisfaction of hearing God's word and doing it; rather than live thus, the world tries to nourish itself on what is by comparison mere pigswill.

In this context 'worldliness' is plainly something very different from what it has often been confused with, involvement in specific 'worldly' activities. About these it is unwise and even impossible to legislate. Individuals may seek guidance in such passages as I Timothy 4:4; I Corinthians 10:25f, 6:12; Matthew 5:28f; Romans 4:13–23; I Corinthians 8:8–13; Romans 14:10; 12:1.

We have already seen that many human activities which are not directly linked with salvation may nevertheless glorify God, as Paul says in I Timothy 4:4f. Yet like everything else in creation they may both draw men away from God and become occasions for a truly 'worldly' spirit.

The danger of worldliness is that we breathe it in every waking moment of our lives. The mass media channel it into our homes—a source of danger that some Christians have understandably but mistakenly tried to evade by excluding newspapers, radio and television. Its assumptions are largely unquestioned in our society. Jesus said that the quality of human life does not depend on possessions; but a million respectable voices declare Him a liar since our economy depends for its existence on the insatiable covetousness of 'consumers' who are conditioned to break the tenth commandment. 'Flee fornication' warns the Holy Spirit, but, pornography apart, our society has trivialised, packaged and commercialised sex to a degree that humanists as well as Christians deplore (Romans 2:14f is still true). In a 'Christian' country things are made worse by apostate churchianity as well as lukewarm believers who try to justify the inexcusable. No wonder there is talk among young people of the need for an 'alternative' society based on different values. How tragic that such a society cannot be recognized wherever there is a local church.

It would be unbiblical and naive to think that going into a 'holy huddle' will deliver Christians from worldliness. Anger, pride, self-seeking, love of comfort, self-indulgence, jealousy— all these can be seen not merely in religious circles but within Christian churches and among active workers, who sometimes engage in really vicious in-fighting and backbiting. Self-indulgent middle-class Christians have not always resisted the temptation to condemn as worldly or unbecoming comforts or practices which do not tempt them simply because they enjoy alternatives which they believe to be unobjectionable.

Conclusion

Certainly the Spirit of Jesus, who in His life and death could be seen to have 'overcome the world', should disclose itself in a life style radically different from that of the world. In work, marriage, government, creativity and every other activity comprised in the mandate of Genesis 1:26, Christians are called to live positively and attractively (not so much as 'christians' but) as mature men and women, the first fruits of a new order (Jas. 1:18). There could be no better recommendation of the gospel. While Christians are not to let the world squeeze them into its mould (as J. B. Phillips renders Rom. 12:12a), the remedy does not lie in being squeezed into another religious or 'spiritual' mould. Through inner transformation by the Spirit they can discover in experience what it is to do God's will in God's world.

13

The Church's Educational Ministry to Youth

MARY BATCHELOR

'Go ... and teach' was a last commission of our Lord to His apostles and teaching is therefore an inescapable part of the church's ministry. Although this chapter is largely concerned with some aspects of the church's work among young people, we recognize that the watertight age divisions that exist in our society are artificial. The gift of teaching is given by the Spirit for the building up of the whole church and her educational ministry must extend to every age-group if the command of the Lord is to be fulfilled.

Youth and the Church

As an institution the church is not generally popular with the under-twenty-fives. A recent survey in the United Kingdom showed that only eleven per cent take her teachings seriously and only eight per cent attend church for any other purpose than weddings, christenings and funerals. Many sections of the church are deeply concerned about the need to present the teaching of Christianity in such a way that young people will see its relevance for their own lives. Some have taken steps to put new teaching schemes into action. At its union in 1972 the United Reformed Church appointed three full-time secretaries to deal with the education and training of youth and a full-time Teacher Training Officer. The Anglican Church has full-time diocesan advisers for Sunday School work to whom any church can apply for advice and guidance. The Baptist Union set up a study group to inquire into the relation of the child to the church. Whatever our view of the action taken we must share both the concern which it reflects and the determination to share in the task of presenting as effectively as possible to the new generation the faith delivered to us.

Before we discuss *how* we are to teach we should be certain *what* we are trying to teach. The Authorised Version 'teach' of Matthew 28:19 is rendered by later translators 'make disciples of'. The injunction then is not merely to impart a body of knowledge but to foster in others a response which will lead them to become followers of Christ themselves. To bring the child to a conversion experience is not the sum total of the task, although it is a vital stage in the process. No teacher, of course, can bring about the response of faith by his own skills. 'We are simply not able to give the child this thing called Christianity. All we can do is to create the conditions, in the child and in ourselves, which make it possible for the Spirit to act.'[1]

When conversion takes place the task of teaching remains just as necessary. The overall object remains the same—to communicate a way of life, to make Christ relevant within the context of the child's or teenager's developing personality and experience. The Bible is of course our stock in trade but presented not as a source of proof-texts but to help young people to understand, handle and apply the Scriptures for themselves. Thus equipped their Christian education will have scope to continue long after they have parted from us.

There are two different groups of young people for whom the church has responsibility, the children of church members and those who attend Sunday School or church services from outside the fellowship of the church. At some stages these groups may be taught together, but in general their educational needs will differ greatly and these differences must be recognized and catered for if both are to reach the same goal of spiritual maturity.

Youth from a Christian Home

For the children of those who are members of the local church, education begins in the home. Most often it falls to the lot of the mother rather than the father to pray with the child, tell him Bible stories and answer his questions. Because women have played a silent role in the life of the church they have in too many instances abdicated their spiritual responsibility. They have ceased to think out their faith, if indeed they were ever encouraged to begin doing so. The early instructing of a child requires patience, care and clear, prayerful thinking and is of paramount importance. But parents should not feel alone in this difficult task. The church has a responsibility to work in partnership with parents to bring up the child in the Christian faith. Some denominations which adopt a dedication service for the families of those in their fellowship include in it a promise to be made by the congregation that as church members they will share in the responsibility of bringing them up in the 'discipline and instruction of the Lord'. The teaching in the church should be an extension and strengthening of the teaching in the home. 'The church and the home are not in competition. Both are gifts from God to be enjoyed and to be entered into responsibly. Their respective roles are complementary. There is a sense in which it may be said that the Christian family is a church and without qualification the church may be viewed as the family of God. Both are ruled by Christ. In both, Christian love, worship and service must find a place. Only as the church helps parents to fulfil their role as creators and leaders of Christian families will it in turn be strengthened by the presence of those families within its life.'[2]

In spite of all the advantages for a child of a Christian upbringing, there are certain concomitant dangers to be avoided by parent and teacher. It is popular in some educational circles to call all Christian teaching indoctrination; while we would strongly deny the use of such a term for wholesome instruction, it is still unfortunately true that children are sometimes brainwashed into acceptance of evangelical belief. Of course, it is right that young children should be given a clear framework of right and wrong. Some indulgent and well-meaning adults might deny children these standards, but it is generally recognized that clearly defined limits for permitted or forbidden behaviour are needed in child-rearing in order to provide a sense of security, this quite apart from Christian ethic. Naturally the Christian parent or teacher will base his moral framework on Bible standards. But in the desire to make right and wrong crystal clear and to inculcate what are considered 'sound' attitudes and responses it is sometimes a temptation to force the child into the mould of the adult's own party line. An imposed, ready-made ethic, presented without room for argument or reasoning, cannot adequately meet the growing child's needs. If he is biddable or plain lazy, he may in fact carry over into adult life the pattern of ready-made beliefs received from family or church; but he is not likely to be a mature person or one who is prepared for the changing situations he will encounter. More likely, the indoctrinated child will abandon the whole scheme of Christian things along with other signs of parental dependence when he leaves the church or family fold.

As Christian educators, our task, in fact, is to limit to the minimum the dogmatic statements taught, and to differentiate clearly between what is lawful and what is expedient. In the realm of manners the child has to learn that putting his knife in his mouth is not 'naughty' in the sense that rudeness or greed are. In the spiritual realm likewise he must learn the relative importance of different matters of belief and practice, and develop a true sense of spiritual values. Adolescents are perspicacious in any case and will usually be painfully or angrily aware of the substitution of inessentials and tradition for the teaching of Christ. Parents and churches who have failed to be aware of their own adherence to custom and party shibboleth may seriously stumble younger Christians. Perhaps it is time to think out afresh the essentials of our faith in the light of Scripture, not usage, and under the guidance of the Holy Spirit.

In the Epistle to the Galatians Paul explains the necessary part played by law until Christ came and faith was revealed. A child in a Christian home often follows the same road from law to grace. In teaching such children it is possible to hinder the progression by too strong an emphasis on law. As sinful mortals we find it a good deal easier to lay down the law

147

than to demonstrate the grace of God. We sometimes witness the joyful release experienced by a person who is converted to Christ from a non-Christian background. Yet children who grow up in Christian home and church may never enter into such a sense of freedom and forgiveness. From early child-hood we may set up a chain reaction of failure and guilt that they may be psychologically unable to break in later years. Somehow we must demonstrate the liberating power of Christ's forgiveness and the freedom to be found in Him in *our* lives. We must also demonstrate forgiveness in our relationship to them if we are to lead them into the freedom with which Christ has set us free.

Youth Without a Christian Heritage

Children who come to Sunday School or church services from a home background divorced from Christian teaching require a very different approach and emphasis. Instead of over-familiarity we are faced with an ignorance we can scarcely reckon with. In the first place, there is complete ignorance of a spiritual dimension in life. Those who teach religion in day school are aware of a blank incomprehension of spiritual realities in a teenager whose upbringing has been wholly devoid of religion of any kind. It is necessary somehow to make such children aware of a God-dimension, though it may often seem like describing colours to the blind or tunes to the tone deaf. It follows that they will have no concept of reverence or worship in relation to God. Somehow they must be made conscious of His presence in church or Sunday School as well as being told the fact of His existence.

We must also be aware of their ignorance when we try to explain the Christian faith. William Neil[3] quotes the advice of an army commander to a group of padres. 'Remember that the chaps don't talk your ordinary language' he said. 'Don't use jargon. Words like love, joy, peace mean one thing to you and another to them. Words like gospel, salvation, Holy Spirit and Holy Trinity mean nothing to them at all.' We need then to allow for both their ignorance of the technical terms of the Christian faith and of the varying connotations of a familiar word. A great deal of preparation and hard thinking is required to make ourselves understood. The format, illustrations and, above all, the laguage of *The Good News Bible* (TEV) will go a long way to help the teacher in the process of communicating. For the young people themselves it will overcome the blanket of incomprehension thrown over much teaching by use of the much-loved but largely defunct language of the Authorised Version.

Some local churches have adopted a new name or time for the Sunday School in order to give it a new look. If our teaching is to bear fruit a basic change of method is also needed in some cases. Haphazard recounting of Bible stories or repeated gospel appeals are not a good diet for children either at five or fifteen. Many branches of the Christian church recognize the need for a carefully devised course to cover the needs of the child over a number of years. The British Lesson Council, composed of representatives of a number of various Nonconformist denominations, produces a syllabus and lesson notes to be used for children of all age groups as well as adults. Many of our Sunday Schools use magazines such as Scripture Union Lessons. Ideally a local church could devise its own syllabus which could dovetail with a teaching scheme for the whole church, but it would involve an enormous amount of co-ordination, hard work and skill.

The Need for Training

We live in an age of specialists, yet our mode of church life is largely based on non-specialization. In our emphasis on the priesthood of all believers and the adequacy of the Spirit's instruction, we have often undervalued and even mistrusted the expert. Scriptural truth that the Spirit gives gifts to whom He pleases has sometimes been debased to an assumption that any male member of the church is capable of fulfilling any function in the church. Such an all-inclusive approach has led to slackness in the careful appointing of men and women for the task of teaching young people. H. L. Ellison[4] comments on this: 'It is by no means unknown for the

149

older teenager to be asked to take a Sunday School class, though it was known that he had no experience and had shown no sign of teaching ability. It is time that we realized that all teaching is a gift, and that the younger the child the more difficult it is to teach.' The report of the Baptist Union inquiry makes the same point: 'For too long it has been customary to encourage young people to teach children in the younger departments ... we believe that those who take responsibility for teaching should be committed members and mature Christians and that the church should endeavour to release them from other duties so that they may concentrate on this vital form of service.'[5]

Even when a person feels called to the task of teaching young people and shows some gift for the work there is still a need for training. A knowledge of present educational methods and some elementary child psychology is essential if teaching is to be effective. A generation ago children were subjected to learning processes very different from those adopted in most schools today. To say that it is unnecessary for the church to follow the fashion and dictates of modern educationists is to miss the point. We need to communicate not only in words that will be understood but in ways that are accepted if our teaching is to have the maximum impact. Many churches have among their members trained teachers who could help in the training of Sunday School teachers. In a local church which is by no means exceptional I recently counted seven professional teachers who covered between them every category of age and ability from infants to students at a college of education. Many other local churches must be as well provided and those who cannot call on their own members to run training sessions could make use of local courses by organisations such as Scripture Union or Scripture Press.

We began by saying that the educational ministry of the church should extend beyond the stages of childhood and adolescence. Too often the work has become sadly fragmented. The teachers in Sunday School and Bible Class need to be vitally involved in the whole life of the church, and those not directly involved with teaching need to be informed and co-operating in the work among young people. There needs, too, to be a satisfactory transition for the young convert from the Bible Class to the general teaching given in the church for its members. At present, little or nothing is done in many churches to prepare such people even for baptism and church membership. From apostolic times catechetical instruction was given, and today many branches of the Christian church hold courses lasting from a few weeks to as long as three years in order to teach the doctrines of Christian belief and the personal implications of faith in Christ. Other churches provide written material, with leaflets prepared for group leaders and participants. Too often in our local churches all that is required is a single 'interview' to satisfy the elders that a genuine commitment to Christ has been made. What is expected is a brief statement of the theology of the atonement rather than an understanding of the requirements of Christian discipleship. Here is an area in which there is need for specific teaching schemes in some churches as well as for more written material.

Truth in Relationship

Our Lord was the perfect teacher because He always de-monstrated in His life and actions the lessons He taught. The quality of the teacher's life is more important and effective than the most successful techniques. 'An experience-centred Christian education can be provided only by those whose daily living is evidence of the way in which they have come to terms with the gospel and with themselves. . . . We suggest that all church members should consider the significance of personal relationships in Christian nurture and should be reminded that, whether or not they are appointed teachers, they are teaching the children by their daily contacts in home and street as well as church.'[6] So the whole church, willy nilly, is drawn into the task of teaching. What the children learn in theory in their classes the church demonstrates in practice. They are taught the love of God in Christ as they

151

study the gospels; but it is the caring, loving community of the church that makes that love a reality.

Within the scope of this chapter it is imperative to mention—though without space to do more—the wider educational ministry of the church outside the walls of home or church building, in the universities, colleges and schools. Whether or not the subject taught is specifically religious, a Christian teacher brings to the classroom both the values and graces of Christian faith. We tend not to reckon with the fact that our own children and those in our Sunday School are constantly subjected to a view of life and learning that is implicitly or sometimes explicitly humanist and anti-Christian. The Christian teacher's attitude both to education and to his pupils will reflect Christian ideals and concepts. The Christian teacher will care about the total development of the child—spiritual as well as mental, physical, emotional and social—and he will show that care in his relationship with the child. In encountering someone who shows him love in this deepest sense the child will encounter Christ, even though he may never enter the doors of a local church.

NOTES

1 Rosemary Haughton, 'The Foundation of Religious Teaching' quoted in *Religious Education*, ed. P. Jebb

2 *The Child and the Church: A Baptist Discussion*

3 *The Plain Man Looks at the Bible*

4 *The Household Church*

5 *The Child and the Church*

6 *Ibid.*

14

Lessons from the Early Church

F. F. BRUCE

When the editors of this volume invited me to contribute something to it in the form of lessons to be learned from the primitive era of the church, it seemed to me that this was an exercise which I had undertaken several times across the years, ever since J. B. Watson persuaded me to write a chapter on 'Church History and its Lessons' for *The Church: A Symposium*, which appeared under his editorship in 1949. For several reasons, however, I was glad to accept their invitation. A further twenty-five years' reflection on the beginnings of the Christian church has taught me lessons of whose existence I had no inkling when I wrote that earlier chapter. The relationship of the New Testament church with the church of the present day is a subject which, in one aspect or another, I have frequently discussed with Cecil Howley, and it appears most appropriate that I should say something about it in a symposium designed to do him honour. It is natural that some of the illustrative material in what I write should be drawn from that tradition of church order which he and I share; it is perhaps also natural that some examples should be adduced from that venerable tradition which forms part of his Southern Irish heritage. Whether the resultant essay provides serious *lessons* is for others to say: I take leave to present at least some *thoughts* from the early church.

Which Church ?

If Peter and Paul could come back to earth for a week or two—say, to one of the cities, such as Rome, which they knew in their day—where would they find most congenial fellowship on a Sunday morning? If this question were asked

153

in some mixed audiences, the questioner would have to beg
his hearers to answer one at a time; otherwise there would be
a deafening babel of conflicting replies. Many of the replies,
however, could be reduced to a common formula: With *us*, of
course! But wherever they might go today, they would
probably find the company and the proceedings strange, and
that not only because of the changes in language and culture
that the passing centuries have brought.

But if they did come back and find congenial fellowship,
would they necessarily find it in one and the same company?
We may assume that they would, but we might be wrong.
There was one famous occasion, in Syrian Antioch, when
Peter found the company kept by Paul inconveniently in-
clusive, and sought a more restricted fellowship—although
this, we must admit, was not so much from his own choice as
from a desire not to make life too awkward for his friends
back home in Jerusalem. One of those friends was James, the
Lord's brother—and it appears, incidentally, that when they
were in Jerusalem Peter and James did not belong to the
same household church. If Peter belonged to the group which
met in the house of Mary the mother of John Mark, he knew
that James and 'the brethren' (whoever they were) met
somewhere else (Acts 12:17). Since the church of Jerusalem,
according to Luke, was several thousand strong, it could not
meet as a whole in one place; and of the household groups
which it comprised, those would count themselves particularly happy which had an apostle or comparable leader in
their membership. Moreover, human nature being what it is,
in the first century or the twentieth, we should expect that
some of these groups would attract those who preferred more
cautious and conservative ways while others (like the
Hellenistic groups to which Stephen and his associates had
belonged before persecution drove them out) would be more
liberal and adventurous.

Hypothetical questions are not very fruitful. Let us ask one
of a more factual sort. Where did Peter and Paul go when
they visited Rome? Not to St Peter's or St Paul's, we may be
sure, for in AD 60 there were no Christian basilicas on the

Vatican hill or by the Ostian Way. Paul indeed was not in a position to 'go' anywhere when first he came to Rome; he had to remain under house-arrest, and other people came to him. It would not be surprising if Paul's tenement flat became the locus for a small and variable household church during his two-years custody in Rome, over and above the many household churches already existing in the city. Some purists would discourage us from referring to the 'church' of Rome in AD 60; the Letter to the Romans, they point out, is not addressed to a city church, as several of Paul's other letters are, and a number of separate household churches receive mention in Paul's list of greetings in Romans 16:3–16. At the same time, there must have been sufficient cohesion, or at least communication, between the various groups for Paul to be confident that his letter would reach 'all God's beloved in Rome, who are called to be saints' (Romans 1:7).

It was probably to one of the household churches in Rome—one with Jewish antecedents and associations—that the Letter to the Hebrews was written a few years after Paul's Letter to the Romans. And a century later Justin Martyr, asked by the city prefect where he gathered together his disciples, replied that it was 'above one Martin, at the Timiotinian Baths'; 'and', he added, 'all this time (and this is my second visit to Rome) I know no other meeting than his.' Justin's professed ignorance of any other meeting may simply mean that he had never been to any other; in any case, the meeting which Justin and his friends frequented could have been much more like a philosopher's school than the average household church in Rome.

Before they had church buildings of their own (as they had in several places by the end of the third century), Christians met for worship in private houses, a special room in such a house being sometimes set apart for Christian meetings. Of this we have clear evidence in some of the most ancient Christian sites in Rome, for example in the substructure of the basilica of San Clemente. It is a moving experience for a Christian visitor to reflect that Christian worship has been carried on continuously on such sites from the days of the

155

imperial persecutions, over a period of seventeen or even eighteen centuries.

It is almost an article of faith with Protestants that Roman Catholic worship represents a sad falling away from the practice of apostolic times. But when a Roman Catholic visits Rome, he is impressed with the sense of historical continuity. On this and that site, he feels, century by century, the holy mysteries of the faith have been celebrated from the remote beginnings of Roman Christianity, and in the same language. It is not easy to persuade him that the form of Christianity which he knows, and which he believes to be attested by the most ancient Christian monuments, is a corruption of apostolic Christianity. If Peter came back to Rome, he may think he would be quite at home in (say) Santa Pudenziana, built on the site of the house of Pudens where, according to tradition, he lived for seven years.

Well, we may say, *we* know better. But do we? Change there certainly has been during these eighteen centuries— change sometimes for the worse but sometimes for the better. But the general *pattern* of worship today in any one of these ancient churches is recognizably the same as it was by the end of the second century. Are we then bound to conclude that there were greater changes in the first two centuries of the faith than there have been since then? If so, when did these changes take place? To locate them in the 'tunnel' period between AD 75 and 175 is easy, just because our inadequate knowledge of the details of church life in that period makes it difficult to disprove many statements that are made about what happened then. At the end of the period we are confronted by the catholic church, the catholic ministry, the catholic canon and the catholic faith in a more developed form than they had at the beginning of the period; but the roots of this fourfold development are present before we enter the tunnel.

Is such development a bad thing or a good thing?

Departure or Development?

When I was in my teens I read with great interest a

paperback which came into our home, entitled *Departure* (1925). The author (G. H. Lang) indicated the main thrust of his thesis more fully in the sub-title: 'A warning and an appeal addressed by one of themselves mainly to Christians known as Open Brethren'. I was not unduly troubled by the current tendencies which he deplored; indeed, in so far as I knew anything about them, I may even have approved of some of them. What fascinated me chiefly was the use which he made of early church history. I realize now that he leaned too heavily on Edwin Hatch's Bampton Lectures on *The Organization of the Early Christian Churches* (1880), with his theory that the bishop was in origin the principal financial officer. But one fact emerged quite unmistakably, above all others, from Mr Lang's comparative study: when a modern movement starts out with the deliberate intention of reproducing the life and order of the apostolic age, it will before long reproduce the features of the *post*-apostolic age, such as standardization of worship, ministry and doctrine, formalizing of inter-church relations, and so forth. These features might be regarded by some as natural or even desirable developments; what the author of *Departure* thought of them is shown by the title of his book. In fact, some of them were of the nature of development and others of the nature of departure. Development and departure are two different things and should not be confused. Development is the unfolding of what is there already, even if only implicitly; departure involves the abandonment of one principle or basis in favour of another.

More recently, Roy Coad's *History of the Brethren Movement* (1968) has enriched us in many ways with the remembrance of things past, and not least by quotations from a work nowadays known only to a few—Henry Craik's *New Testament Church Order* (1863)—which anticipated B. H. Streeter's *The Primitive Church* (1929) in pointing out that the New Testament provides adumbrations of episcopalian, presbyterian and congregational church order, alongside 'what may be described as less systematic than any of the above organizations.' This is a matter of simple truth, but it was highly unfashionable to acknowledge such a simple truth in the middle of the nineteenth century. 'It appears to me', said Craik, 'that the early churches were not, in all places, similarly constituted.' A consideration of the constitution and government (or non-government) of the churches of Jerusalem, Antioch, Corinth and Rome in the apostolic church would confirm his statement.

Paul indeed seems to have attached some importance to preserving a certain measure of uniform practice throughout his churches. In writing to the volatile church of Corinth he urges it more than once to restrain its tendency to deviation and bring its practices into some kind of conformity with those of 'the churches of God' (I Cor. 11:16) or 'all the churches of the saints' (I Cor. 14:33b). While he was primarily concerned with churches of his own planting, in which he was entitled to institute his own ruling (I Cor. 7:17), he appears to have had in mind the wisdom of maintaining in his own churches some degree of conformity with churches not of his planting, especially with the mother-church of Jerusalem and her daughter-churches. It is plain that he was always anxious to foster fellowship between his Gentile mission and the Jerusalem church, and this fellowship would have been strained even more than it was if the Gentile churches used unfettered discretion (not to speak of indiscretion) in matters of ecclesiastical order. Arnold Ehrhardt once pointed out that Paul was 'one of the greatest assets for the Church at Jerusalem', despite Jerusalem's misgivings about him, because under his influence, when not by his personal action, non-Jerusalem versions of the gospel were brought into line with that which he and the Jerusalem leaders held in common.[1] Even so, diversities in primitive church order can be discerned; they would have been greater but for Paul's policy, arising out of his concern to maintain unity not only within churches but between churches.

But Henry Craik was not content with drawing attention to *diversities* of primitive church order; as Mr. Coad also reminds us, he recognized a *development* of order within the New Testament. Again, in saying that in apostolic times 'a more fully developed church organization and official position were introduced as occasion called for them,' Craik was saying something which has only to be stated to be recognized as true. But if it is true, it rules out any idea that one uniform and unchangeable pattern is to be discerned in the apostolic writings and followed by all churches which wish to be scripturally ordered. The one uniform pattern which can indeed be discerned in the New Testament is the pattern of flexibility which facilitates instead of impeding the free movement of the Spirit as he makes provision for the churches and their members as and when the need arises.

Spirit and Structure

'Like Jordan,' wrote R. B. Rackham in expounding the Pentecostal narrative of Acts 2, 'the full and plenteous flood of the Spirit "overflows all its banks" (Josh. 3:15). At first the worn-out vessels of humanity cannot contain it; and there is a flood of strange and novel spiritual experiences. But when it has worn for itself a deep channel in the church, when the laws of the new spiritual life are learnt and understood, then some of the irregular phenomena disappear, others become normal, and what was thought to be miraculous is found to be a natural endowment of the Christian life.'[2] This should be borne in mind on the recurring occasions when God does a new thing in the church, and those who are responsible to maintain decency and order are disturbed by the incursion of unfamiliar and unpredictable practices.

There was probably a time in the early days of the Brethren movement when, with the conscious abandonment of a fixed liturgy, one never knew in the course of a meeting for worship what was going to happen next. Nowadays, with the fixation in many places of another (albeit unwritten) liturgy, one often knows only too well what is going to happen next. Some of us may think that our familiar order of worship provides adequate room for the liberty of the Spirit, but by use and wont we have come to expect the Spirit to move in well-recognized ways. It might cause no little surprise in some places, and possibly even dismay, if (for

159

instance) at a communion service a couple of young people contributed to the worship by singing an impromptu duet, with or without guitar accompaniment. In other places, however, their contribution might be accepted spontaneously in the spirit in which it was offered.

It is, in fact, a mistake to set the charismatic and institutional aspects of church life in opposition the one to the other: both are necessary. The flood waters of the Spirit will drain away ineffectively without vessels or channels to contain them and convey them to the areas where they are most needed; the vessels or channels, for their part, require to be filled with the life-giving water if they are not to be empty and useless. The institutions or structures may be traditional, but they are none the worse for that if they serve a useful purpose; on the other hand, to maintain institutions or structures for their own sake when they have outlived their usefulness is traditionalism of the wrong kind.

What sort of institutions or structures, then, should be regarded as most desirable? Light and flexible ones, which can be maintained without undue cost and labour so long as they are serviceable, and be dismantled without regret when something more suited to the needs of a new day comes along. Some institutions are allowed to grow so old and venerable that the idea of scrapping them is unthinkably sacrilegious. Consider as an example the historic episcopate, which sometimes proves to be a very awkward obstacle in the path of Christian unity. At one time the historic episcopate was a safeguard against the intrusion of subversive doctrine and other dangers; does it fill this role today? If it does, good and well; but some churches which preserve it are not more obviously free from the menace of erroneous teaching and practice than are others which live happily without it.

Something to the same effect may be said about the historic formularies in which the church has traditionally confessed her faith. The ancient creeds are worthy of Christian veneration and acceptance since, as Article VIII of the Anglican Thirty-nine Articles of Religion puts it, 'they may be proved by most certain warrants of holy Scripture'.

But the language of some of them is too technical (and technical in a fourth and fifth-century sense) to be readily understood by many Christians who recite them today. It may be reasonably answered that the Christian who recites the Nicene Creed is not so much expressing his personal faith as confessing his membership in the church whose faith is set forth in these terms; but it is better when the question 'Understandest thou what thou sayest?' can receive an affirmative reply. More than that: experience shows that the regular recital of the ancient creeds in a Christian community does not guarantee that it will be more immune from false doctrine than other communities in which they are rarely or never recited. To judge by fragments of confessional statements embedded in the New Testament writings, Christians of apostolic days got along with fairly simple affirmations of faith, which were yet explicit enough to exclude denials of Christ's lordship or of His incarnation. If we inherit or devise confessions of faith, let them at the same time conserve the apostolic witness and be flexible enough to accommodate whatever light the Lord may yet have to break forth from His holy Word.

Unity in the Apostolic Church

Such unity as was maintained in first-century Christianity was not ensured by a superstructure. There were the apostles, indeed, but we should not exaggerate or idealize the extent of their authority. Paul did not care to have the authority of the Jerusalem apostles imposed by their emissaries on his Gentile churches: after his contretemps with Peter at Antioch he could never be sure that one of them might not yield to pressure as (in his judgment) Peter did and sell the pass. He had no thought of imposing his own authority outside the limits of his commission—we can see how careful he is in this regard when writing to the Roman church, which was 'another man's foundation'—but his restraint was not always matched by others, and there were those who questioned his apostolic status and did their best to undermine his authority even in his own mission field.

There was, of course, a basic unity of faith and life. Paul himself acknowledges that the outline of the gospel—Christ died, Christ was buried, Christ was raised the third day—was common ground to himself and the Jerusalem leaders (I Cor. 15:3–11). And in an alien world anyone who called Jesus Messiah or Lord or Son of God would be greeted by Christians as one of themselves. But the extremist judaizers would have qualified as fellow-Christians by this test, and so probably would many of the gnosticizers. If some of the latter were so 'way out' as to say 'Jesus is anathema' (I Cor. 12:3)—meaning perhaps that the heavenly Christ was all that mattered now, while the earthly Jesus was no longer of any account—they would scarcely have been recognized as true believers by the Christian majority.

The New Testament bears ample witness to the centrifugal tendencies in apostolic Christianity: we have only to think of the tensions between Jewish and Gentile Christians, between legalists and libertarians, between the rank and file who were content with the 'simple gospel' and the spiritual élite who preferred what they imagined to be more advanced teaching. But it bears ample witness also to the centripetal forces which kept churches and Christians together, and the greatest of these was love. Here we may think of the spontaneity with which the young Antiochene church came to the aid of Jerusalem in time of scarcity and of the readiness with which Paul assented to the request of the Jerusalem leaders that he and Barnabas should go on remembering the poor, readiness which manifested itself on the largest scale in the Jerusalem relief fund which he organized among his Gentile churches. This example persisted in the post-apostolic age. Some churches were outstanding in charitable enterprise, especially the church in Rome. Half a century after Paul's stay in Rome, Ignatius begins his letter to the church there by commending it for its distinction in every noble quality, and above all for its exercising the 'presidency of love' among all the churches—a worthy primacy indeed!

Later in the second century (c. AD 170) Dionysius, bishop of Corinth, wrote to the Roman church and congratulated it on the way in which it kept up its tradition of generosity to churches in need. 'Your blessed bishop Soter has not only maintained this custom but enhanced it by his administration of the largesse distributed to the saints and by the encouragement given by his blessed words to the brethren who come to Rome, addressing them as an affectionate father would his children.'[3]

Principles of Catholicity

This letter of Dionysius illustrates another centripetal force of special interest. He refers to his own church of Corinth as being, like the Roman church, a joint foundation of the two apostles Peter and Paul.[4] Paul would certainly have disclaimed any part in the founding of the Roman church, but he might well have turned in his grave at the suggestion that the Corinthian church was founded in part by Peter. And yet Dionysius's attitude, while it outrages historical fact, reflects a sound instinct, and one which Paul himself would have approved. When, shortly after he founded it, the church of Corinth showed signs of splitting up into parties, each appropriating as its figurehead some name of renown in the Christian world of that day, Paul insisted that such a course was foolish self-impoverishment; all of them were entitled to an equal share in all the leading teachers: 'whether Paul or Apollos or Cephas..., all are yours' (I Cor. 3:22).

It was a mark of the catholic church of the second century (more explicitly, a mark of its catholicity) that it claimed as complete an apostolic heritage as it could. Splinter groups might restrict themselves to one strand in the Christian tradition: the Marcionites might look on Paul as the only faithful apostle and dismiss the Twelve as compromisers with Judaism, while the Ebionites might execrate Paul's name and venerate the memory of Peter and, pre-eminently, of James the Just. But the catholic church included in its comprehensive canon everything that could reasonably be regarded as apostolic, not (as Marcion did) the epistles of Paul only but those of other apostles and apostolic men.

Whatever tensions might have existed in the apostolic age

163

between Peter and Paul or between their respective followers, these were transcended a generation or two later. Clement of Rome, at the end of the first century, and Ignatius of Antioch, at the beginning of the second, give Peter and Paul joint honourable mention in a Roman setting. More than that, the canonical Petrine literature contains a friendly reference to 'our beloved brother Paul' (II Peter 3:15), even if it is acknowledged that some of his writings are difficult to understand and liable to be seriously misconstrued.

This agreement to pay simultaneous respect to Peter and Paul, together with the other apostles, is frequently said to be a symptom of 'incipient catholicism', and it would be point-less to deny this. But incipient catholicism, especially under its German designation *Frühkatholizismus*, is viewed by many theologians in the Lutheran tradition as a deplorable de-clension from the purity of the Pauline gospel, so much so that those New Testament books in which it appears are judged for that reason to be sub-Pauline, post-apostolic and at best deutero-canonical. Other symptoms of this declension are said to be the replacement of a charismatic by an institutional ministry, the extension of the term 'church' from the local congregation to cover the world-wide community of Christian people, the adoption of a codified confession of faith and the recession of the imminent hope of glory at the parousia in favour of dependence on the means of grace presently dispensed through the church and its ministry.

In some measure most of these symptoms are present in the New Testament. But the last-mentioned is not to be found. The church as an institution has not yet become the guardian and dispenser of the means of grace. Even in the Pastoral Letters the church is the witness and custodian of the divine revelation, like Israel in earlier days (cf. Romans 3:2), 'the pillar and bulwark of the truth' (I Tim. 3:15). In these three letters, our earliest manuals of church order, the ministry is indeed institutional but has not ceased to be charismatic. Timothy himself has been 'instituted' by prophecy (I Tim. 1:18) and the Spirit still speaks 'expressly' in the church (I Tim. 4:1), although now perhaps through apostolic writings as well as through the lips of prophets. Certainly in the Pastoral Letters the truth is well on its way to being codified (although primitive confessional fragments have been detected in the earliest New Testament documents) and 'the faith' is now used not only subjectively, of the faith with which Christians believe, but objectively, of the sum of what they believe (as also in Jude 3). But these things are simply aspects of that development which Henry Craik discerned within the New Testament itself. The development did not cease when the latest New Testament document was penned, nor was there any reason why it should. If it be asked further (in the light of what has been already said) how development is to be distinguished from departure, or how it can be prevented from lapsing into departure, the answer may lie in certain criteria which the New Testament writings themselves provide.

One Body, One Faith

Another aspect of incipient catholicism appears in the Letter to the Ephesians. 'In the New Testament', says Ernst Käsemann, 'it is Ephesians that most clearly marks the transition from the Pauline tradition to the perspective of the early Catholic era.'[5] Repeatedly the principles of life and ministry in the local church, as we find them set out in I Corinthians, are universalized in Ephesians. But the universal perspective of Ephesians grows out of something already latent in I Corinthians. While I Corinthians is addressed to 'the church of God that is in Corinth', it is intended also for 'all those who in every place call on the name of our Lord Jesus Christ' (I Cor. 1:1)—primarily, it may be, in the same province of Achaia, but not explicitly and probably not exclusively so. The church throughout the world is one, and its oneness depends on the fact that there is one Spirit, one Lord and one God. But the terms in which this is emphasized in Ephesians 4:4–6 are based on I Corinthians 12:4–6, where the collaboration of all the members for the common good in the local church is a corollary of their sharing 'the same Spirit;... the same Lord; and...the same God'. We might

165

antecedently have expected Paul to think of Christians throughout his mission field as forming a unity. 'Israel after the flesh' did not exist only in local synagogues; it was an ecumenical entity. The synagogue in any place was the local manifestation of the whole congregation of Israel. So with the new Israel: what we might antecedently have expected is confirmed by the evidence in Paul's earlier letters of his deep concern for Christian unity, not only unity among his own Gentile churches but unity which bound them together with the Jerusalem church and the churches of the Jewish mission.

Again, all Christians according to Paul were baptized 'into Christ', not merely into a local fellowship, and thus formed part of one spiritual whole. The Christians in Corinth are reminded that they are Christ's body, and individually members thereof (I Cor. 12:27); similarly those in Rome are told that 'we' (that is, not the Roman Christians only but the Roman Christians in fellowship with other Christians), 'though many, are one body in Christ, and individually members one of another' (Rom. 12:5). But to Paul's way of thinking Christ could no more be parcelled out between the several congregations than He could be divided between the factions within the congregation at Corinth. Language such as he uses to the Corinthian and Roman Christians could not be locally restricted, even if the occasions of his writing to them directed its application to the conditions of local fellowship. All believers everywhere had together died with Christ and been raised with Him; as participators in His risen life they could not but constitute one Christian fellowship. The explicit exposition of the universal church in Ephesians is an unfolding of the significance of Paul's phrase 'in Christ' and all that goes with it. Here too we are bound to recognize authentic development within the New Testament.

The Acts of the Apostles
But there is another New Testament document which displays the features of 'incipient catholicism' more impressively still, and that is Acts. From the middle of the second century

onwards it has been called 'The Acts of the Apostles' not because it records the acts of all the apostles (it does not) but because it does not confine itself to one strand of apostolic tradition. Paul may be the author's hero—although in the only places where he calls Paul an apostle he makes him share the designation with Barnabas (Acts 14:4, 14)—but Peter receives a fair share of attention: indeed, commentators have drawn out the parallels in this work between the 'Acts of Peter' (chs. 1–12) and the 'Acts of Paul' (chs. 13–28). At the Council of Jerusalem, Peter and even James come down in principle on the side of salvation through grace by faith, apart from legal works; and the letter sent to the Gentile churches by the apostle and elders of the Jerusalem church makes appreciative reference to 'our beloved Barnabas and Paul' (Acts 15:25), while Barnabas and Paul, for their part, seem quite happy to accept the stipulations laid down in the letter. Acts certainly gives us the impression that trouble was always prone to break out in Jerusalem when Paul visited the city, but the tension between Paul and the leaders of the Jerusalem church, which can be discerned so pervasively beneath the surface in several of Paul's letters, has left hardly a trace in Acts. In Acts Paul and Barnabas, Peter and James, with their respective associates, appear as a happy band of brothers. On the one occasion when Paul and Barnabas have a sharp difference of opinion, it is on personal grounds, quite unlike the difference at Antioch recorded by Paul, when *even Barnabas*, the last man of whom it might have been expected, was carried away by the 'play-acting' of Peter and the other Jewish Christians (Gal. 2:13).

But when Acts was written, Paul's career was at an end. That career had been marked by trials and tribulations from within the Christian community as well as from outsiders; but all this could now be recollected in tranquillity. This does not mean that an interval of a generation or two must be postulated between Paul's death and the composition of Acts. We ourselves have known highly controversial figures in church life who in old age enjoyed considerable veneration, even on the part of those who had been involved in

IN GOD'S COMMUNITY

controversy with them. At that time of day, and all the more
so after their death, the general feeling was: Why recall the
controversies when so much that is more edifying can be
recorded? The controversy at Antioch was crucial enough
when it happened, and it was still so when Paul wrote to the
Galatians. A few decades later it was ancient history and,
from Luke's point of view, might well remain unmentioned.
It could make no contribution to the purpose for which he
wrote.

The Church's Calling
The church is the dwelling-place of the Spirit, and 'where the
Spirit of the Lord is, there is freedom' (II Cor. 3:17).
Structures of ministry, government and order are of value so
long as they provide vehicles for the free moving of the
Spirit; when they cease to do that, they should be replaced
by more suitable ones. Whatever at any time helps the
church to discharge her proper functions—the worship of
God, the strengthening of fellowship within her membership
and the witness of outgoing and self-giving love to mankind—
that is what matters. When the church thinks more of her
status than of her service, she has taken a wrong path and
must immediately retrace her steps. As the church's Lord was
(and remains) the Man for others, the church must be the
society for others, the community of the reconciled which is
at the same time the instrument by which the reconciling
grace of God in Christ is communicated to the world. All
that enables the church to be this is true development; all
that hinders the church from being this is departure.

NOTES

1 *The Framework of the New Testament Stories* (1964), p. 94
2 *The Acts of the Apostles*, Westminster Commentaries, 14th ed. (1951), pp. 15–16.
3 Eusebius, *Ecclesiastical History* iv. 23.9–11
4 *Ecclesiastical History* ii. 25.8
5 In *Studies in Luke–Acts* ed. L. E. Keck and J. L. Martyn (1966), p. 288

FOR FURTHER READING

General

Brunner, E. *The Christian Doctrine of the Church, the Faith and the Consummation* 1962
————. *The Misunderstanding of the Church* 1952
Cole, A. *The Body of Christ* 1964
Dulles, A. *Models of the Church* 1974
Ellison, H. L. *The Household Church* 1963
Hort, F. J. A. *The Christian Ecclesia* 1897
Küng, H. *The Church* 1967
Lang, G. H. *The Churches of God* 1959
Newbiggin, L. *The Household of God* 1953
Saucy, R. L. *The Church in God's Program* 1972
Stibbs, A. M. *God's Church* 1959
Vine, W. E. *The Church and the Churches* n.d.
Watson, D. K. C. *I Believe in the Church* 1978
Watson, J. B., (ed.) *The Church: A Symposium* 1949
Williams, J. *Living Churches* 1972

The Church in the New Testament

Flew, R. N. *Jesus and His Church* 1938
Johnston, G. *The Doctrine of the Church in the New Testament* 1943
Minear, P. S. *Images of the Church in the New Testament* 1961
————. *Jesus and His People* 1956
Schmidt, K. L. *'Ekklēsia'*, *Theological Dictionary of the New Testament* ed. G. Kittel, Vol. 3 (E.T. 1965) pp. 501–536

Baptism and the Lord's Supper

A. General

Berkouwer, G. C. *The Sacraments* 1969
Clark, N. *An Approach to the Theology of the Sacraments* 1956

B. Baptism

Beasley-Murray, G. R. *Baptism in the New Testament* 1962
Cullman, O. *Baptism in the New Testament* 1950
Flemington, W. F. *The New Testament Doctrine of Baptism* 1948
Gilmore, A., (ed.) *Christian Baptism* 1959
Murray, J. *Christian Baptism* 1952

C. The Lord's Supper

Barclay, W. *The Lord's Supper* 1967
Higgins, A. J. B. *The Lord's Supper in the New Testament* 1952
Jeremias, J. *The Eucharistic Words of Jesus* 1966

Leadership and Authority in the Church

Green, E. M. B. *Called to Serve* 1956
Manson, T. W. *The Church's Ministry* 1948
Moore, W. J. *The New Testament Concept of Ministry* 1956
Morris, L. *Ministers of God* 1964
Saunders, O. *Spiritual Leadership* 1967

169

Worship

Gibbs, A. P. *Worship: The Christian's Highest Occupation* n.d.
Martin, R. P. *Worship in the Early Church* 1964
Moule, C. F. D. *Worship in the New Testament* 1961
von Allmen, J. J. *Worship: Its Theology and Practice* 1965

Pastoral Care and Discipline

Blackwood, A. W. *Pastoral Work* 1945
Lee, R. S. *Principles of Pastoral Counselling* 1978
Oates, W. E. *The Christian Pastor* 1964
————. *Pastoral Counselling* 1974
Thurneysen, E. *A Theology of Pastoral Care* 1962
Turnbull, R. G., (ed.) *Baker's Dictionary of Pastoral Theology* 1967

The Ministry of Women in the Church

Hardesty, N. and Scanzoni, L. *All We're Meant to be* 1974
Jewett, Paul K. *Man as Male and Female* 1975
Knight, G. W., III. *The New Testament Teaching on the Role Relationship of Men and Women* 1977
Swindler, L. *Women in Judaism* 1976
Williams, D. *The Apostle Paul and Women in the Church* 1977

The Church and the Family

Botting, M. *Family Worship* 1971
————. *Reaching the Families* 1976
————. *Teaching the Families* 1973
Feucht, D. E., (ed.) *Helping Families Through the Church* 1957
Parsons, M. *Family Life in a Christian Home* 1972

Christian Stewardship and Church Finance

Church Information Office *Christian Stewardship of Money* n.d.
Olford, Stephen F. *The Grace of Giving* 1972
Rees, Tom *Money Talks* n.d.
Webley, Simon *Money Matters* 1978

The Church and World Mission

Blauw, J. *The Missionary Nature of the Church* 1952
Boer, H. R. *Pentecost and Missions* 1961
Douglas, J. D., (ed.) *Let the Earth Hear His Voice* 1975
Green, E. M. B. *Evangelism in the Early Church* 1970
Stott, J. R. W. *Christian Mission in the Modern World* 1975
Webster, D. *The Local Church and World Mission* 1962
————. *Unchanging Mission* 1965

Christian Unity

Bromiley, G. W. *The Unity and Disunity of the Church* 1958
Hanson, A. *The Meaning of Unity* 1954
Hanson, S. *The Unity of the Church in the New Testament* 1946
Stott, J. R. W. *One People* 1970

The Church and Israel

Benko, S. and O'Rourke, J. J., (eds) *Early Church History* 1972
Campbell, R. *Israel and the New Covenant* 1954
Ellison, H. L. *The Mystery of Israel* 1968
————. In *The Indestructible Jew* ed. F. A. Tatford n.d.
Richardson, P. *Israel in the Apostolic Church* 1969

170

The Church and the World
Anderson, J. N. D. *Into the World* 1968
Berkhof, L. *Systematic Theology* 1953 (on common grace) pp. 432–446
Catherwood, H. F. R. *The Christian Citizen* 1969
Henry, C. F. H. *Aspects of Christian Social Ethics* 1964
Küng, H. *On being a Christian* 1977
Padilla, C. R., (ed.) *The New Face of Evangelicalism* 1976

The Church's Educational Ministry to Youth
Batchelor, A. J. and M. *You and Your Church* 1970
Bullen, A. F. *Parents, Children and God* 1971
Jebb, P. *Religious Education* 1968
Loukes, H. *Teenage Morality* 1973
———. *Teenage Religion* 1961
Old, M. V. *Today's Children, Tomorrow's Church* 1974

Lessons from the Early Church
Bruce, F. F. *The Spreading Flame* 1958
Dowley, T., (ed.) *Lion (Eerdmans) Handbook to the History of Christianity* 1977
Küng, H. *The Structures of the Church* 1965
Schlatter, A. *The Church in the New Testament Period* 1961
Schweizer, E. *Church Order in the New Testament* 1961
Streeter, B. H. *The Primitive Church* 1929

174

INDEX OF SCRIPTURE REFERENCES

184

185